FOREWORD

It is with great pleasure that we present *Baroque Masterworks*, the fourth touring exhibition from the European and American paintings collection of the National Gallery of Canada. This exhibition follows the earlier successful tours of *Impressionist Masterworks*, *Post-Impressionist Masterworks*, and *Masterworks of 19th-Century French Realism*. The works selected here, all dated between 1600 and 1730, belong to a much earlier period in European art, commonly referred to as the Baroque. Never has such a large group of the European masterpieces from the permanent collection toured the country before. Indeed, due to their age and rarity, many of the paintings have never left the Gallery before. During the next year, *Baroque Masterworks* travels to Edmonton, Victoria, Winnipeg, and Halifax. Thus Canadians from coast to coast have an unprecedented opportunity to enjoy their rich heritage of paintings from this key period in the history of Western art.

We are proud to say that these twelve masterworks, which come from all parts of Europe, are drawn from an exceptionally high quality collection of Baroque paintings. Many came to the National Gallery as a result of astute purchases made during the early part of the twentieth century – purchases that would be almost impossible to replicate in today's market – such as Rembrandt's *A Woman at Her Toilet* and Rubens' *The Entombment*. Several others, including Poussin's *Landscape with a Woman Washing Her Feet*, and van Everdingen's *The Rape of Europa*, entered our collection as gifts from very generous donors. The Gallery's commitment to acquiring important paintings for our national collection of European art continues to this day, and is exemplified here by two paintings acquired in 2003 and 2004 respectively, *The Annunciation of the Virgin's Death* by Paulus Bor, and *The Penitent St. Jerome in His Study* by the Pensionante del Saraceni.

Many individuals and groups have worked together to make *Baroque Masterworks* a reality. I would especially like to thank our Board of Trustees for its support as well as the Department of Canadian Heritage for its assistance with the tour through the Canada Travelling Exhibitions Indemnification Program. I would like to extend my appreciation to Mayo Graham, Director of National Outreach and International Relations, for her promotion of the touring program of the National Gallery, and to David Franklin, Deputy Director and Chief Curator, for suggesting this continuation of the series of travelling exhibitions from the European Collections. Stephen Gritt, Chief, Restoration and Conservation Laboratory, was essential to making the project possible. Erika Dolphin, Assistant Curator of European and American Art, organized the exhibition and has written the catalogue that accompanies the tour. For producing it, I would like to thank Serge Thériault, editors Susan McMaster and Danielle Martel, picture editor Colleen Evans, production coordinator Anne Tessier, and administrator Irene Lillico, along with editor Lauren Walker and translator Julie Désgagné. Arline Burwash was of great help with the photographs for the publication, and Ellen Treciokas did the lovely design with the aid of Paul Cavanaugh. Among the many additional Gallery staff who have dedicated their energies to the successful realization of the exhibition are Christine Feniack, with Julie Drapeau and Jodan Drosier, and Daniel Amadei and Karen Colby-Stothart, with project managers Christine LaSalle and Julie Hodgson. They were ably supported by Diane Lafrance-Watier, Danielle Allard, Kristin Rothschild, Fiona Graham, Malcah Sussman, Sue Lagasi, and Gary Rousseau.

Pierre Théberge, O.C., C.Q.
Director
National Gallery of Canada

INTRODUCTION

Baroque Masterworks presents twelve outstanding paintings from the permanent collection of the National Gallery of Canada, which were painted in Europe between 1600 and 1730 and collected through purchase and generous donations between 1936 and 2004.

Despite the common use of the term, there is in reality no single overarching style or painting tradition common to all of Baroque art, nor, indeed, to the paintings brought together here. "Baroque" in the context of this exhibition simply means art produced between the Renaissance and the Neoclassical period. The featured masterworks were painted by artists working in different countries, and in different social, economic, political, and religious climates. El Greco and Vouet lived and worked in the Catholic monarchies of Spain and France, respectively. Poussin lived in Rome and produced erudite paintings for an elite group of private collectors. Rubens travelled widely, painting large allegories glorifying the virtues and endeavours of European princes. Rembrandt and van Everdingen both worked in the Protestant Dutch Republic (today The Netherlands), but even within the same country, very different painting styles existed alongside each other. While Rembrandt exploited the expressive qualities of a loose and free brushstroke – in sometimes highly personal works – at the end of his career in Amsterdam, van Everdingen, working in Haarlem and Alkmaar, painted classical subjects with a very finished and precise brushstroke, giving his paintings an almost porcelain quality.

Though futile to search for one style common to all Baroque art, it is possible to discern certain new attitudes to picture making that began to emerge at the beginning of the seventeenth century, and that affected the work of disparate artists working in varying styles. Foremost among these was an interest in naturalism. Caravaggio was a driving force behind one manifestation of this trend, and several artists featured in this exhibition, such as Rubens, Vouet, and the Pensionante del Saraceni, were influenced directly by his innovations, having travelled to Rome early in their careers. In his day, both artists and collectors were thrilled with Caravaggio's use of un-idealized models: of ordinary folk who looked as if they had just walked off the streets of Rome straight into the studio. Artists in particular found Caravaggio's use of a single-source raking light very effective at giving the composition a sense of drama. Vouet's *The Fortune-teller* and the Pensionante del Saraceni's *St. Jerome* show well how Caravaggio's followers used and developed these innovations. The strong light delineates form and enhances the sense of looking at real three-dimensional bodies. Anecdotal details from everyday life also heighten the feeling of peering in at a small slice of reality. St. Jerome's studio is full of items that seventeenth-century viewers would recognize from their own homes, including books, candle holder, scissors, and hourglass. Exploring the dramatic use of strong light and contrast was not, however, the sole purview of artists who knew the work of Caravaggio. Both Rembrandt and Lievens used it to great effect to spotlight the protagonists in their compositions. Lievens' *Job* is visually isolated in a pool of light, which delineates his naked and aged body in such a graphic way that his psychological woes seem all the more poignant and palpable.

Job is also a notable example of a second feature common to the Baroque era: artists were not merely interested in the accurate transcription of the physical world. They wanted to affect the viewer on an emotional level, to make each composition dynamic, and give it a life-like, immediate vitality that would leap beyond the frame and speak directly to the person standing there. A common technique was to blur the distinction between real and fictive space, effectively drawing the viewer almost physically into the painting – a trick that works as well today as it did then. For example, in Rubens' *Entombment*, the lid of the sarcophagus upon which the figures stand juts out diagonally into the space of the viewer, and the body of Christ looks as if it is being laid down right in front of us. Rubens' painting is a copy of a much larger work by Caravaggio that hung immediately above an altar, thus giving the remarkable impression that Christ's body was being lowered onto the actual altar table during Mass. In this way, time and movement were effectively suggested in the painting, contributing considerably to its life-like quality and believability. The fallen chair Mary uses as a *prie-dieu* in Paulus Bor's *The Annunciation of the Virgin's Death* plays a similar function, drawing us into the picture. Vouet's *The Fortune-teller* also speaks directly to the viewer, but in a different fashion. The woman having her fortune read looks out of the frame right at us, acknowledging us, and implicating us in the conspiracy to dupe the gypsy, who is having her pocket pilfered by one of the scallywags behind her.

Alongside the interest in the natural world was a continued respect for the classical one. The knowledge of ancient art and architecture, revived in the Renaissance, had grown and become more widespread during the seventeenth century due to systematic study by classical scholars and formation of great collections by nobles and connoisseurs. The paintings of Poussin and van Everdingen in this exhibition offer two quite different expressions of classical taste. Poussin's *Landscape with a Woman Washing Her Feet* probably depicts Hercules' enslavement to Omphale, an esoteric tale taken from ancient mythology. At the time, the painting appealed both to the viewers' intellect, through their knowledge of arcane mythology, and, as a rumination on penance and remorse, to their emotions and moral character. On the other hand, van Everdingen's rendition of the ever-popular tale of *Jupiter and Europa* was simply a reworking of a dramatic love story and a wonderful excuse to paint semi-nude women in a manner suitable to decorate the walls of a wealthy home.

New types of painting, such as landscape, "low-life" scenes, and still-life, developed as independent genres during the seventeenth century. This was a result of both the emerging interest in naturalism, and the dramatic growth in the number of private collectors wanting to buy works of art appropriate in size and subject for their middle-class and wealthy homes. The works by Poussin, Vouet, and Rembrandt are good examples of paintings like these made for a private collector, rather than a church or palace. With the rise in the mercantile economy, buying paintings was no longer the sole purview of the church and monarchy. Artists, especially in the Dutch Republic, where a merchant class was booming, no longer needed patrons to commission individual works, but could instead sell finished works directly from their studios. The market for small private paintings, often of secular subject matter, also expanded in response to the diminished need for religious works to decorate churches, at least in the Protestant state of the Dutch Republic, which eschewed images in churches. However, Catholic populations were not entirely suppressed even there, and there were many "closed" or clandestine churches where altarpieces were still used, especially in Utrecht. Bor's *Annunciation of the Virgin's Death* may be an example of this.

Of course, in Catholic countries there was still a need for altarpieces and other religious paintings for churches. We do not know if El Greco's *St. Francis* ever hung over an altar, but it seems likely that it was meant for a church since in 1900 it was hanging in the choir of the church of Cristo de las Aguas in the town of Nambroca, near Toledo. Devotional paintings meant for use in the home existed during the Middle Ages and Renaissance but were made solely for the elite. As with other types of paintings, such pictures became more widely available in the Baroque, partly as a result, no doubt, of the Counter Reformation's extolling of the practice of private worship. Cavallino's *St. Dominic* was probably used in such a fashion.

Baroque naturalism was not one of rigorous objectivity. Artists, collectors, and worshippers in Catholic churches never lost their disposition to look for symbolic meanings in nature and art. The allegorical tradition lived well into the eighteenth century, as can be seen in Crespi's *Allegory of the Arts*. Even Jordaens' *A Young Cavalier Executing a Levade*, a *modello* (model) for one of a series of tapestries depicting different aspects of horsemanship, has an allegorical dimension. A prince or noble who owned and hung these tapestries was, in addition to warming and decorating the palace or villa, making a comment on his own suitability to his position in society. One complete set of tapestries, for example (now in the Kunsthistorisches Museum, Vienna), was bought for the Viennese Imperial Court in 1666 for Emperor Leopold I. Like the emperor, one needed wealth, prestige, and leisure to afford horses, stables, and lessons. And the whole point of learning the levade – a seemingly effortless but exceedingly difficult movement – was to convey the authority and ability of the rider.

Above all, the twelve remarkable pieces brought together in *Baroque Masterworks* reveal the growing number of functions paintings came to perform during the seventeenth century, from the traditional altarpieces of Bor and private devotional paintings of Cavallino, to the secular subjects made for a growing group of private collectors, such as the low-life scenes of Vouet and the classical landscapes of Poussin. Baroque art may be characterized, paradoxically, by an absence of stylistic unity, but this exhibition demonstrates that the Baroque era produced unusually powerful images that still speak to us today.

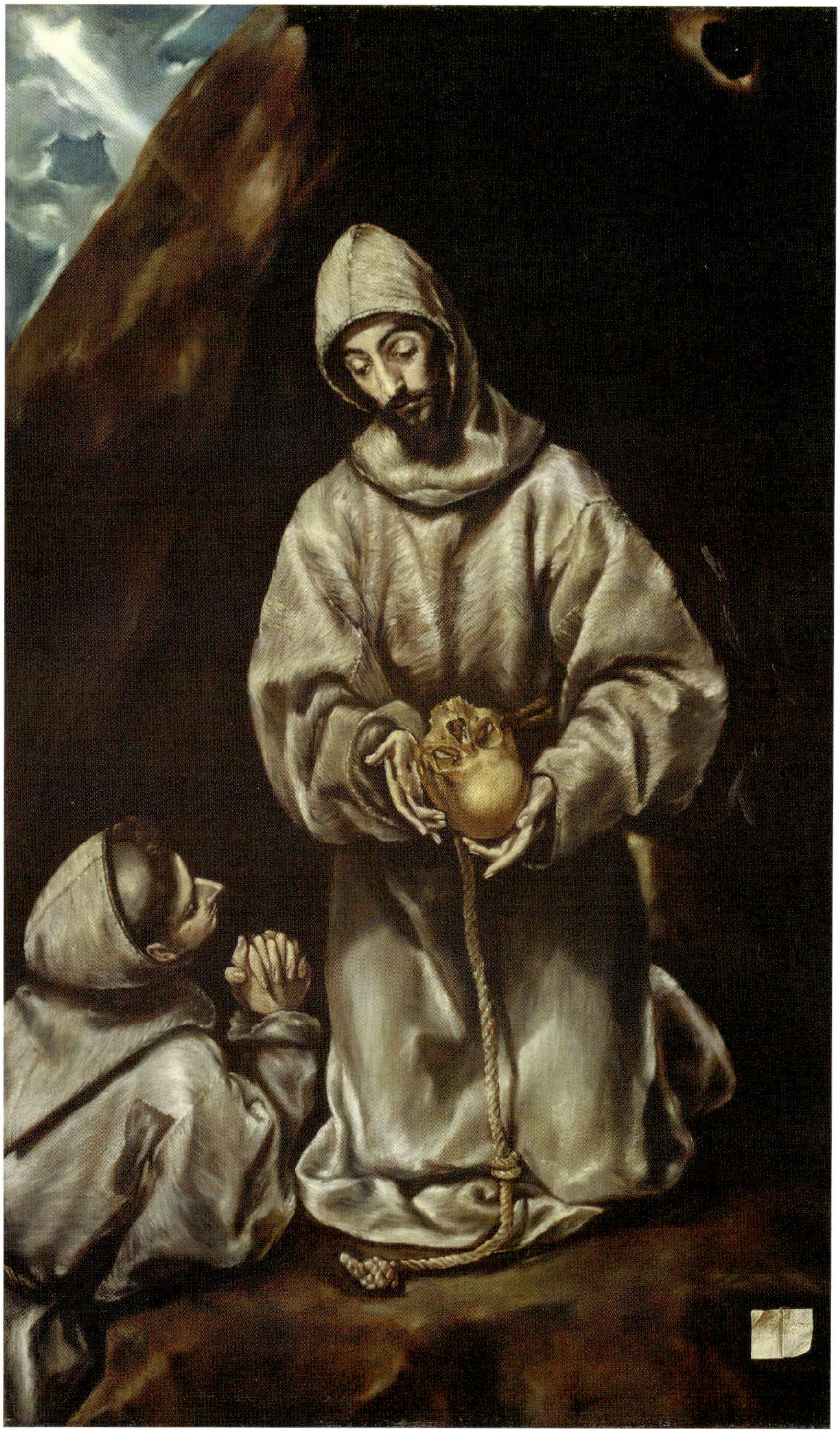

El Greco (Spanish, 1541–1614), *St. Francis and Brother Leo Meditating on Death,* c. 1600–05, oil on canvas, 168 × 103.2 cm. Purchased 1936 (4267)

Think about life and death: that is what St. Francis (c. 1182–1226) set out to do when he retreated to a cave on Mount Alverna in Tuscany to fast and pray. El Greco's painting may lead the modern viewer to similar thoughts. Everything draws our eyes to the human skull placed dead centre: St. Francis looks down at it; his hands gently encircle it; the belt-cord of his habit points up to it; Brother Leo bends his gaze and praying hands towards it. We do not need to be steeped in Counter-Reformation Catholicism to understand this cogent reminder that death awaits us all.

The search for a personal spiritual life and a mystic union of the soul with God through contemplative prayer formed a cornerstone of religious reform in Spain in the 1600s.[1] *St. Francis and Brother Leo Meditating on Death* is a painting made for private devotion, to help the believer meditate on mortality, repentance, and the vanity of earthly pursuits. Indeed, St. Ignatius of Loyola (d. 1556), one of the foremost saints of the Counter-Reformation, recommended using an actual skull.[2]

St. Francis was revered for his rigorous practice of ascetism and meditation; his spiritual union with Christ is represented here by the lesion on his right hand, one of the stigmata (wounds of Christ's crucifixion) he received while on Mount Alverna. Devotion to St. Francis grew rapidly during the seventeenth-century, especially in Spain, and the demand for images like this was considerable. The artist, his workshop, and followers painted some forty versions and copies of this particular image, of varying quality. The National Gallery's painting, by El Greco himself, is one of the earliest, and came from a design he made in the 1580s.[3] The image was so popular that an engraving was made after it by Diego de Astor to produce affordable prints for a wider public.

El Greco was born in Candia, Crete, trained in Venice and Rome, and settled in Toledo in 1577. There he established a successful career painting altarpieces, devotional paintings, and secular paintings (mostly portraits) for the church and private patrons from a local circle of intellectuals, many of them clergy. Although sometimes considered quintessentially Spanish, El Greco was proud of his cosmopolitan heritage. When he signed his paintings, he did so in Greek, as he has done here, on a *trompe l'œil* piece of paper "affixed" to the canvas with a dab of red wax at the bottom right. It reads: δομήνικος Θετοκόπουλος ἐποίει, which means "Domenikos Theotokopoulos made it." Curiously, the moniker El Greco (The Greek), used by both his Spanish contemporaries and us today, combines the Spanish *El Griego* with the Italian *Il Greco*.

In *St. Francis and Brother Leo Meditating on Death*, St. Francis looms over the viewer. The space around him is flattened, and the figure presses precariously upon the picture plane, as if he could easily topple forward. El Greco's rejection of classical perspective – of a naturalistic rendition of three-dimensional space – and the exaggeratedly elongated bodies of his figures, make his paintings distinctive. These "unnatural" aspects of El Greco's style make his work difficult to place within the history of European art, which is most often understood as a progress to ever greater realism, beginning in the Renaissance and ending with the advent of photography. Some historians have even thought the painter was subject to mystical visions or that he had problems with his eyesight.[4] The discovery of El Greco's writings has made it clear that his rejection of the symmetry, balance, and proportion of the classical tradition[5] espoused by such masters as Raphael and Michelangelo was a deliberate aesthetic choice on his part. By compressing space, he heightens the emotional effectiveness of his paintings, as we see here, where he forces the presence of both saint and skull palpably and unavoidably onto the psyche of the viewer.

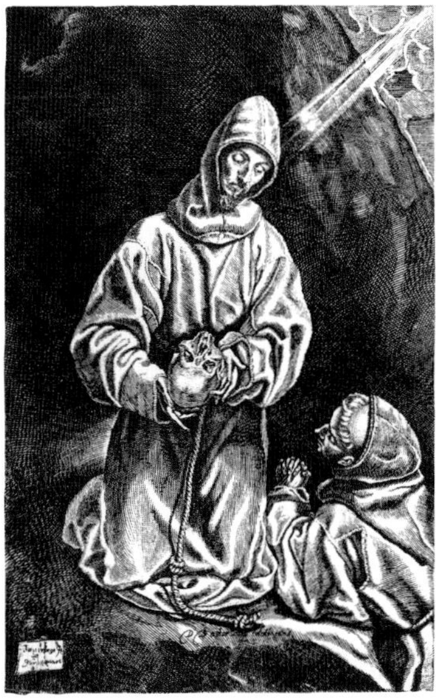

Diego de Astor after El Greco, *St. Francis and Brother Leo Meditating on Death*, 1606, engraving, 23 × 14.8 cm. Biblioteca Nacional, Madrid (42372)

Like Caravaggio and Vermeer, El Greco was largely forgotten until the nineteenth century, when enthusiastic critics suddenly "discovered" him as a great innovator who forecast modern art, a proto-Cubist or -Expressionist. Recent scholarship places him firmly within the context of late sixteenth- and early seventeenth-century Toledo, and the sympathetic circle of intellectuals, friends, and patrons within which he lived and for whom he painted.[6]

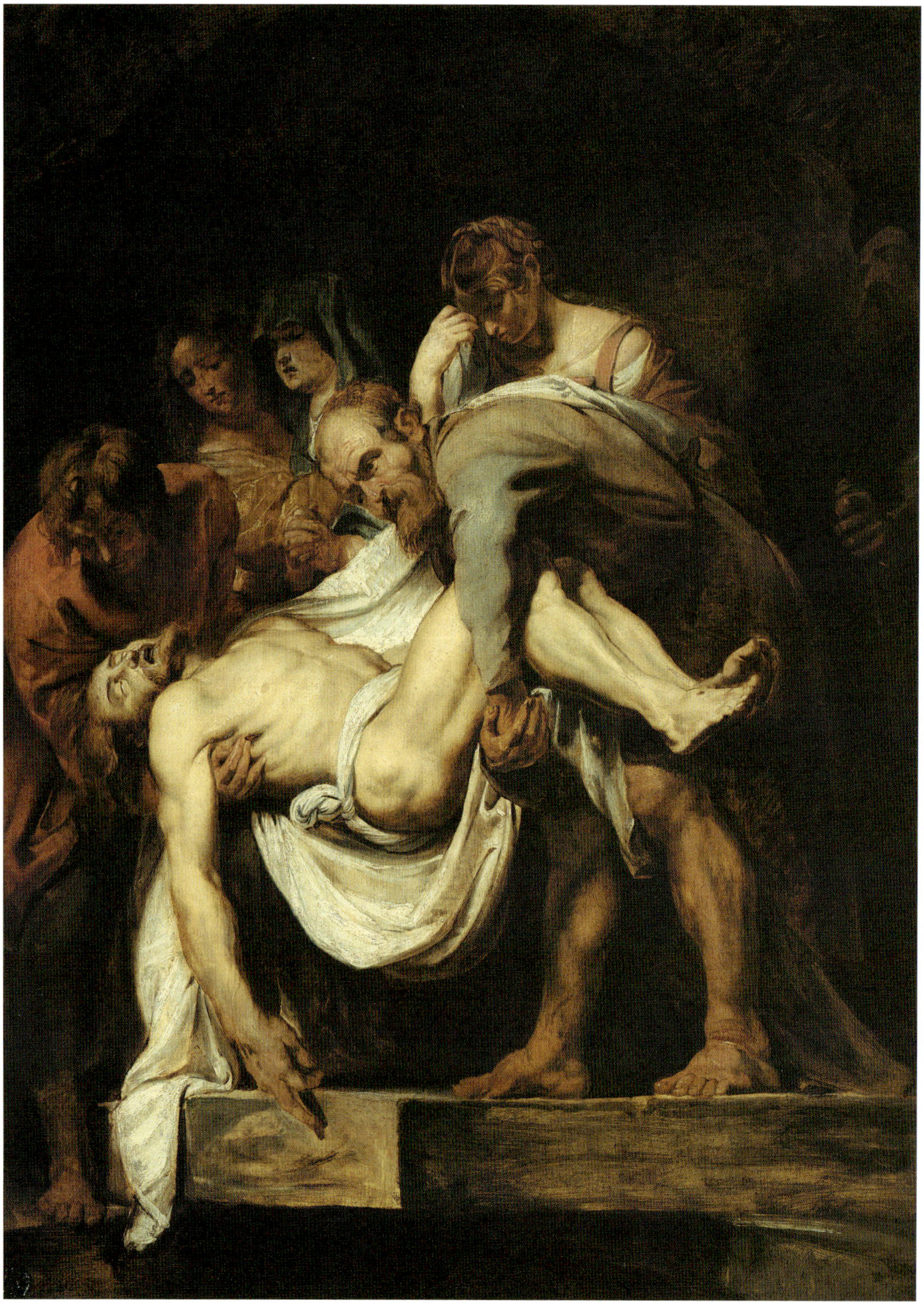

Peter Paul Rubens (Flemish, 1577–1640), *The Entombment*, c. 1612–14, oil on oak, 88.3 × 66.5 cm. Purchased 1956 (6431)

This modest, yet powerful and moving painting by Rubens is a copy after an altarpiece of Caravaggio's – but not a simple replica. At first glance the two paintings look rather similar; however, Rubens made changes that suggest he felt challenged to "improve" the Italian master's work. Such a strong sense of competition and ambition is not surprising in the artist who was to become the foremost painter of the Northern Baroque. A gifted and erudite artist, an astute businessman, and a diplomat, Rubens enjoyed an extremely successful career, coming to know and work for most of the crowned heads of Europe.

Rubens encountered Caravaggio's altarpiece early in his career when, like many Northern artists before him, he travelled to Italy in 1600 to study the celebrated sculptures of ancient Rome and the works of such Renaissance masters as Michelangelo, Raphael, and Titian. Of his contemporaries, Rubens admired a select few, notably Caravaggio and Annibale Carracci, the two leading figures of the Italian Baroque. While in Rome, most northern artists could find work only as itinerant painters or landscape specialists, so it was quite a coup when Rubens received the commission to paint the high altar of the church of Santa Maria in Vallicella (also known as the Chiesa Nuova) in 1606. Once there, he would have had ample time to study Caravaggio's *Entombment*, which had been installed in the chapel of the Pietà in the same church three years earlier.

Interestingly, the style of Rubens' painting suggests he did it not on the spot, but several years after his return to Antwerp in 1608. No drawing for the painting made by him in Rome has been discovered, and it is possible Rubens did it from memory. He certainly boasted that he was capable of such a feat. When rebuked by a colleague for spending too much time just looking at the great Roman art works instead of drawing and painting copies after them, Rubens retorted: "I believe that I have better retained that which I have looked at, than you who have drawn it."[1]

Caravaggio's *Entombment* is large, some three by two metres, and would have made a striking impression on Rubens when he saw it in the chapel of the Pietà. It hung directly above the altar, and because Caravaggio does not represent the empty tomb waiting beneath to receive the body of Christ, St. John and Nicodemus appear to lower Christ directly onto the actual altar table below. The altarpiece thus makes visible the doctrine of Transubstantiation: the belief, promulgated during the Counter-Reformation, that during Mass the bread and wine are literally converted into the body and blood of Christ.

Rubens' work is much smaller, and consequently more intimate, yet it is clear how much he admired Caravaggio's sense of drama and realism. In both paintings, strong light contrasts dramatically with a dark background to give the burial party a markedly three-dimensional quality, making the figures tangible and their grief palpable. In Rubens' version, the composition is less static and the figures have more breathing space, so that the narrative is easier to read. He deepens Caravaggio's shallow stage by subtly toning down the contrast and letting some light fall on an arched space behind, where he adds a turbaned man looming in the shadows. By bringing St. John's foot down a step on the left of the painting, Rubens adds a sense of movement both forward and downward. He also clarifies the composition by representing only one visibly distraught young woman. Caravaggio's inclusion of the woman with her arms raised in despair is emotionally powerful, but leaves the viewer wondering whether she or the anguished woman holding a cloth to her eye is meant to be Mary Magdalen.

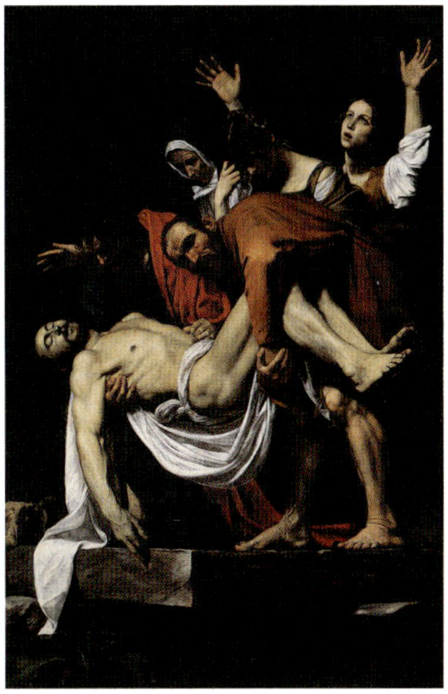

Michelangelo Merisi da Caravaggio, *The Entombment of Christ*, c. 1601–04, oil on canvas, 300 × 203 cm. Vatican Gallery, Rome (40386)

Due to the small scale of Rubens' panel, some have suggested it was meant for private devotion. It is more likely that the painting was a formal exercise in composition, in which Rubens worked out ideas to be developed elsewhere.[2] He was very much in the habit of making "free copies" after other artists: an estate inventory of 1640 indicates he made these for his own benefit and study rather than for sale, since he kept most, if not all, in his house in Antwerp.[3] Throughout his career Rubens referred to the works of others in his own paintings, sometimes lifting elements entirely, but most often reworking and adapting them. In this way, he stayed in constant dialogue with other artists, situating himself in the mainstream of a continuing and developing tradition of art.

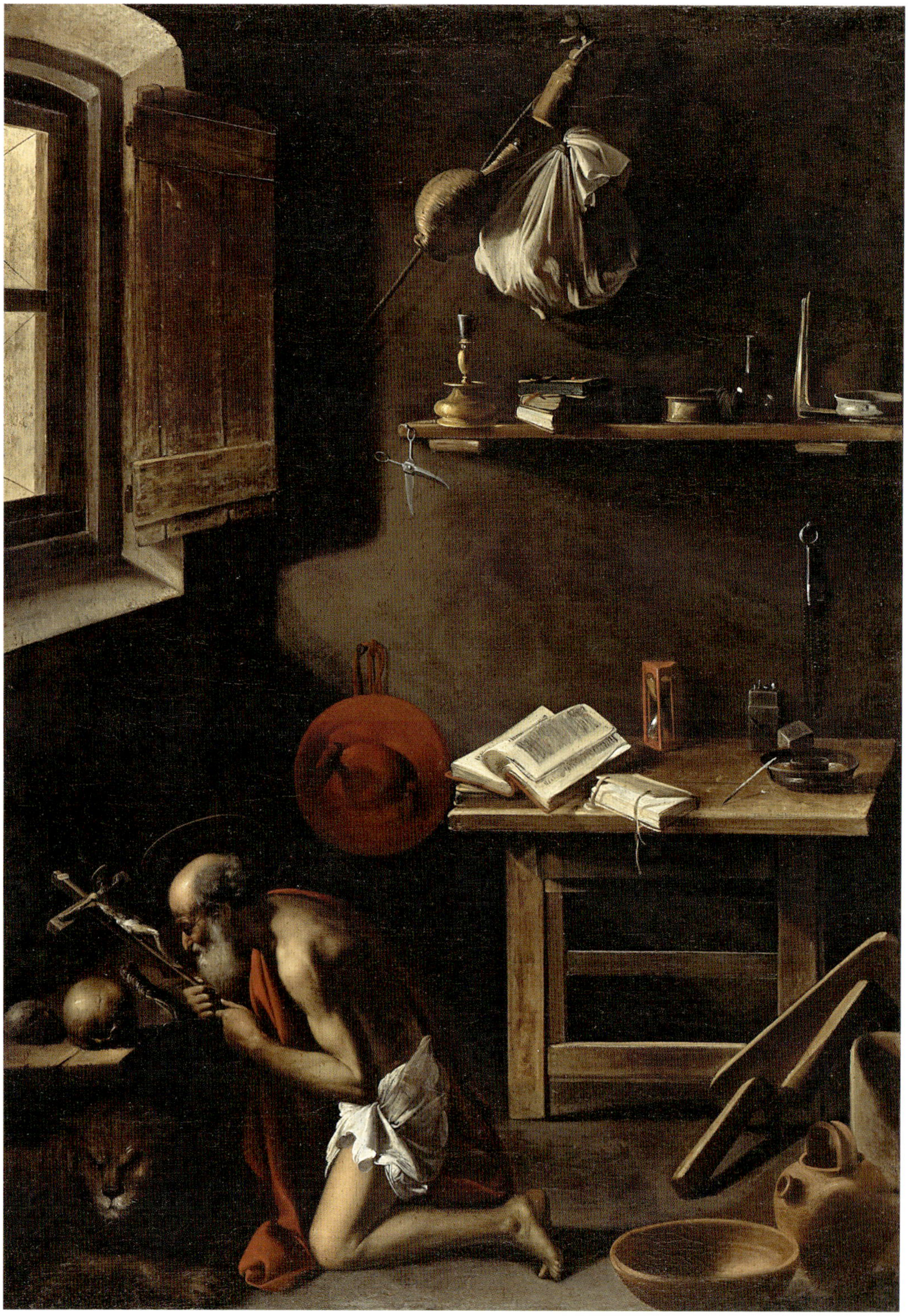

The Pensionante del Saraceni (Italian, active c. 1610–1625), *The Penitent St. Jerome in His Study*, c. 1615, oil on canvas, 171.4 × 122.4 cm. Purchased 2004 (41455)

This touching and evocative painting of a humble St. Jerome deep in prayer, by a mysterious painter known as the "Pensionante del Saraceni," is a major discovery for the history of Baroque art in Rome. Neither the artist's real name nor birthplace is known. However in 1943 the highly respected scholar Roberto Longhi recognized a distinctive artistic personality behind a small group of paintings that were close in style to the work of Carlo Saraceni, but which had a distinguishing French or northern European accent. Longhi gave this elusive artist the sobriquet of "Pensionante del Saraceni" – literally "Saraceni's lodger" or "tenant." Saraceni painted in a Caravaggesque style in Rome during the first decades of the seventeenth century. An ardent Francophile, he dressed in French clothes, spoke the language fluently, and had several French students and followers.

Despite today's research techniques, it is not unusual to encounter a seventeenth-century painter whose identity remains unknown. The style of the Pensionante's pictures indicates that he had direct knowledge of Caravaggio's early works and was painting in Rome during the 1620s and 1630s. The Pensionante responded not only to the immediacy of the emotional content in Caravaggio's work, but also to his vigorous naturalism and tenebrous lighting, consisting of strong contrasts of light and dark created with a beam of raking light entering an interior space. Yet the Pensionante also had a penchant for detail that is often associated with the art of northern Europe. Albrecht Dürer – a Northern artist highly influenced by Italian art – displays this characteristic in his celebrated engraving of *St. Jerome in His Study*. In fact, the interior still-life elements of shelves holding books, candle-holder, scissors, and hourglass, which we see in the Pensionante's rendition of St. Jerome's study, are reminiscent of Dürer's print.

St. Jerome (342–420), one of four Latin Fathers of the Church, was a learned man who retired as a hermit to the Syrian desert for four years while he studied Hebrew. He later translated the Old and New Testaments into Latin. St. Jerome is most often portrayed as a scholar at work in his study, or as a dishevelled and partly naked penitent in the desert, kneeling before a crucifix, holding a stone with which to beat his breast, and with a skull and hourglass (symbols of mortality) lying nearby. The Pensionante has combined both versions here by placing a penitent St. Jerome, deep in prayer, in a corner of his study with his books and writing implements left abandoned on the table behind. Caravaggio painted several versions of St. Jerome in which he concentrated on the figure itself, omitting much of the setting, whether desert or study. The Pensionante's rendering of a haggard and barely clad St. Jerome, with his wrinkled face, grey hair, and bony body all revealed in a strong light from the left, is clearly derived from Caravaggio.

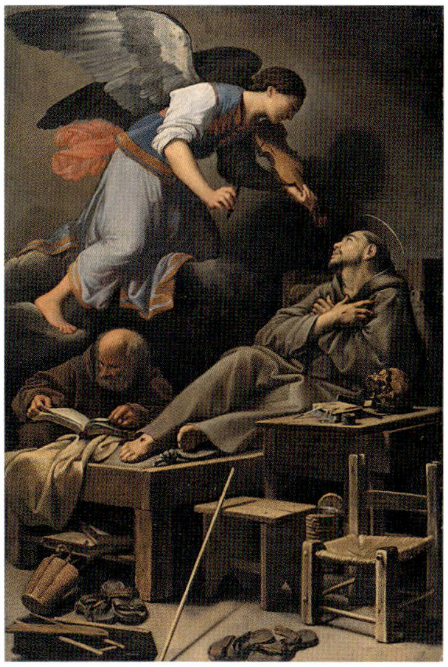

Carlo Saraceni, *St. Francis in Ecstasy*, c. 1615–20, oil on canvas, 242 × 165 cm. Alte Pinakotek, Munich. Photo: Artothek

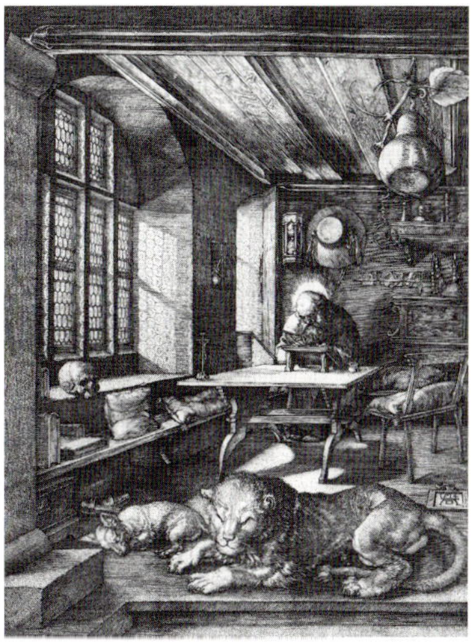

Albrecht Dürer, *St. Jerome in His Study*, 1514, engraving, 24.9 × 19.2 cm. British Museum, London

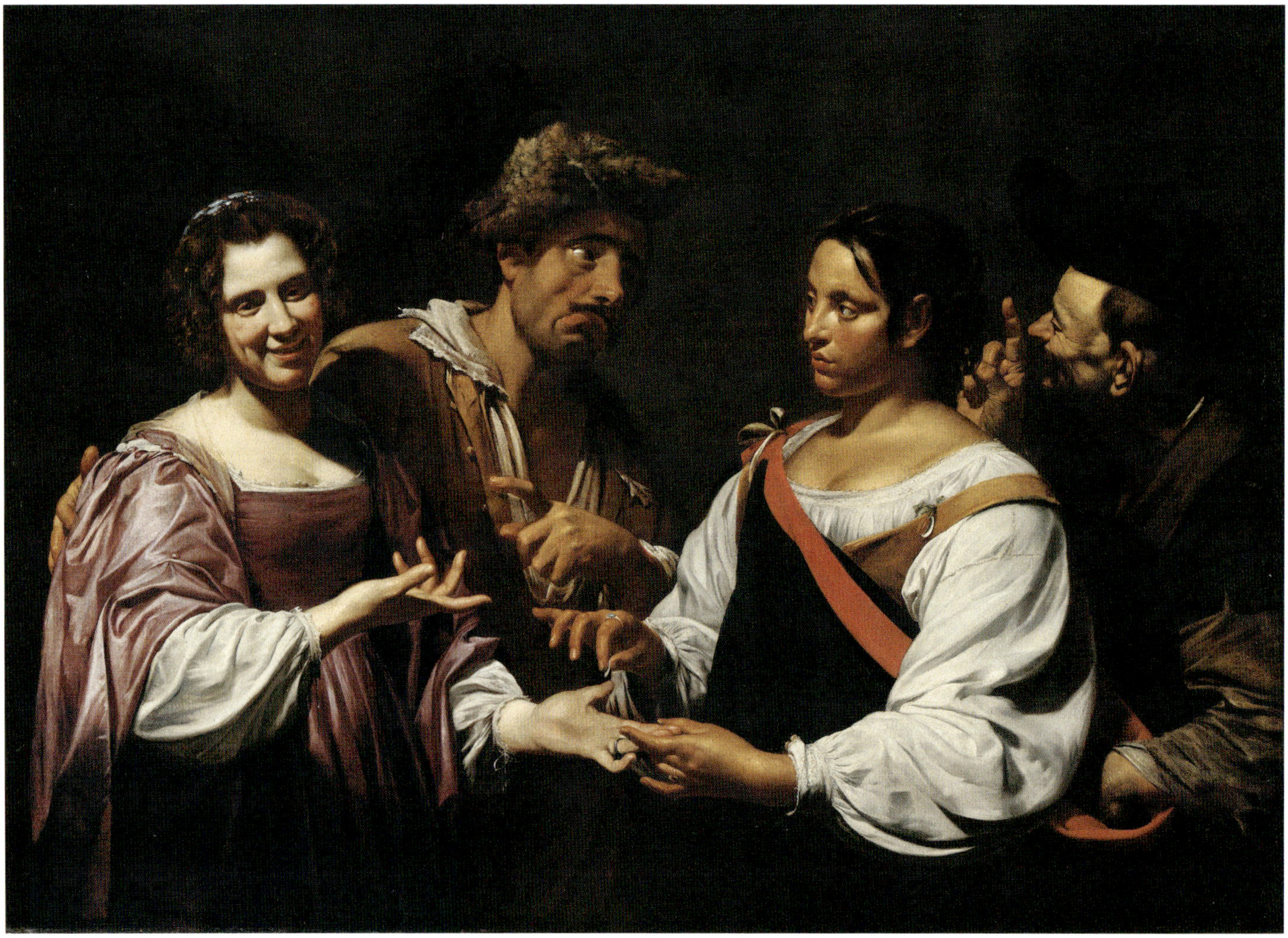

Simon Vouet (French, 1590–1649), *The Fortune-teller*, c. 1620, oil on canvas, 120 × 170.2 cm. Purchased 1957 (6737)

Gypsies, along with rogues and ruffians of all sorts, were a common sight on the crowded and often violent streets of seventeenth-century Rome, jostling for space and easy marks. Paintings of cheats and charlatans – and gypsies were invariably classified as such – became wildly popular in the city after Caravaggio painted two famous works, *The Cardsharps* and *The Fortune-teller*.[1] The latter narrates a straightforward deception: a pretty gypsy has so beguiled a naïve young man with her charm that, while holding his palm to read his fortune, she surreptitiously slips the ring off his finger without him noticing. Caravaggio's followers, Vouet among them, immediately began to paint ever more complicated and nuanced variations on the theme. Vouet's rendition turns the table, and the gypsy herself becomes the subject of deception and thievery. She makes no attempt to pinch the very obvious ring from the hand of the young woman for whom she is telling a fortune, and remains unaware of the rogue behind her who has stuck a hand into the folds of her cloak to steal something. Interestingly, the gypsy does not read the woman's lifelines, but uses another method of prophecy, one that involves holding a coin above the palm. Allegedly, the higher the value of the coin, the more accurate the prophesy, and the coin was sometimes awarded to the gypsy afterward as payment.[2]

The fortune-teller in Vouet's painting is easily identified as a gypsy by the long heavy cloak she wears over one shoulder and under the other, a style of garment described in contemporary costume books as part of typical gypsy attire. Although not in the physical centre of the composition, the fortune-teller provides the narrative fulcrum. Exotic and pleasing to the eye, she is the most appealing character of the group. The two ruffians are scruffily dressed in dirty clothes. The woman having her fortune read wears a fashionable dress, but her grinning, overly rouged face and inelegantly coiffed hair suggest she might be a courtesan; certainly an upper-class woman would not have ventured out into the streets of Rome without a chaperone. She must be in on the scam, since she looks directly at the viewer and points to the gypsy being duped, as if to say, "How humorous life is when one who claims to tell fortunes cannot see her very own destiny." The original owner of the painting would have enjoyed the beauty of the exotic gypsy on the one hand, and the irony of the cheat being cheated on the other.

Vouet's gypsy, like Caravaggio's, is beautiful and serene, but the other three characters give his painting a burlesque tone not found in the master's version. Their gesticulations and broad grins – or frown, in the case of the man in the middle – bring to mind stock street theatre figures from the commedia dell'arte. Indeed, comic plays and novellas of the time often depicted the Roman underworld as a dangerous yet glamorous placc, where tricksters and scoundrels were admired for their craftiness. There was so much interest in the subject that a broadsheet illustrating all of the varied tricks used by beggars and street sellers, *Le Barrarie del Mondo* (The Swindlers of the World),[3] was published around 1590.

Born in France, Simon Vouet became the leading painter in Paris during the first half of the seventeenth century, but he had established his reputation earlier while he was in Rome from 1614 to 1627. There, in addition to painting scenes like the *Fortune-teller*, he made commissioned altarpieces and portraits for aristocrats, and was elected to the prestigious position of president of the Roman Accademia di San Luca.[4] The *Fortune-teller* demonstrates how, during his first years in Rome, Vouet, like many others, was affected by the compelling power of Caravaggio's naturalism, and how he adopted both his use of low-life subjects and his dramatic lighting effects. Interestingly, Caravaggio set his genre scenes in fairly bright interiors, using his characteristic tenebrist lighting only in his religious paintings, whereas the Caravaggisti tended to set all their subjects in dark interiors lit by a raking light. By the time Vouet returned to France, he had developed an eclectic style incorporating the lighter, more decorative palettes of Guido Reni, Domenichino, and Giovanni Lanfranco, a style highly admired by Parisian aristocrats, who hired him to decorate their city and country homes.

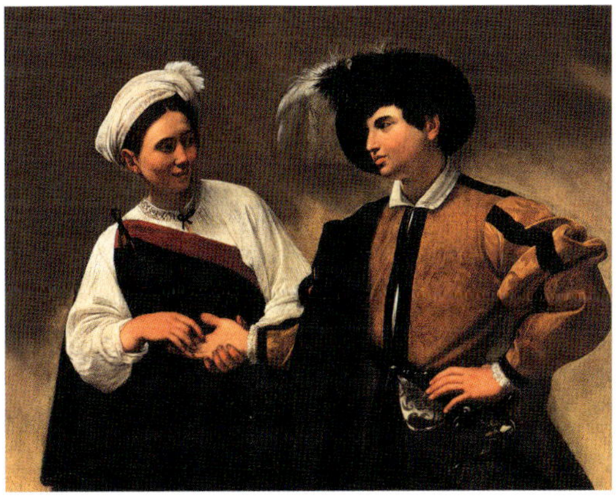

Michelangelo Merisi da Caravaggio, *The Gypsy Fortune-teller*, 1593–94, oil on canvas, 115 × 150 cm. Pinacoteca Capitolina, Rome

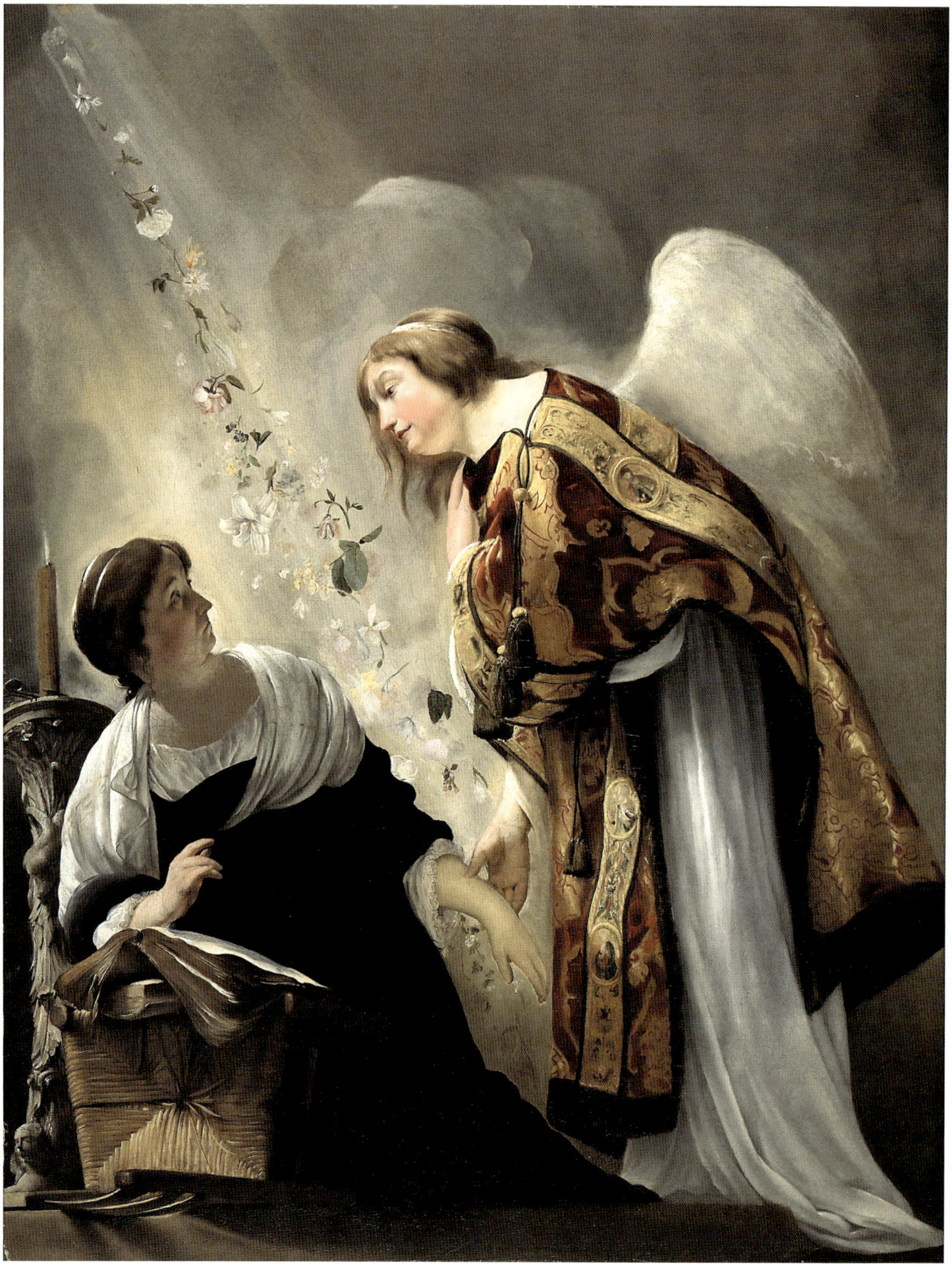

Paulus Bor (Dutch, c. 1601–1669), *The Annunciation of the Virgin's Death*, c. 1635–40, oil on canvas, 203.2 × 157.5 cm. Purchased 2003 (41279)

Paulus Bor's painting is a beautiful rendition of a very rare subject: the annunciation to the Virgin Mary of her impending death. This scene is not found in the Bible, but is described by Jacopo da Voragine in his medieval best-seller *The Golden Legend* (tales from the life of Christ, the Virgin, and the saints, assembled from various sources, including the Apocrypha).

The Annunciation of the Virgin's death is hard to distinguish from the much better-known Annunciation by Gabriel to Mary that she will bear a son named Jesus. But the absence of the Spirit of the Holy Ghost in the form of a dove, and the somewhat advanced age of the Virgin, who wears black, the colour of mourning, lead us to conclude that the archangel here must be advising Mary of her death and not her pregnancy. The burning candle and snuffer are obvious symbols of mortality, appropriate to an episode from the end of the Virgin's life. The remarkable conception of flowers carried down a shaft of light from heaven is of great dramatic and decorative effect, and may refer to a later moment in the story, after the Virgin's Assumption, when the apostles discover her empty tomb filled with flowers. It is true that the archangel does not bear the palm frond described in *The Golden Legend*, which he usually carries in the few other known images of the subject (most of them, like Fouquet's miniature, from the fourteenth and fifteenth centuries). However, unconventional iconography is a hallmark of Paulus Bor, whose extant oeuvre of fewer than thirty paintings[1] is characterized by many enigmatic depictions of arcane subjects. In fact, the subjects of some of his paintings are so obscure that Bor is the only painter known to have illustrated them.[2]

The large size of *The Annunciation of the Virgin's Death* suggests it was made for a place of public worship and not for private devotion. The low vantage point indicates it would have been placed high up on a wall, probably over an altar. Although the Dutch Republic was officially Protestant and images of all kinds were forbidden in its Reformed churches, altarpieces were still commissioned in centres with large Catholic populations, such as Utrecht, where many continued to worship in "hidden" churches. Since Bor's hometown of Amersfoort lay within the bishopric of Utrecht, it is conceivable he provided altarpieces for clandestine churches in the area.

If Bor's painting is an altarpiece, the choice of subject is curious; certainly, it is not as appropriate as the more familiar Annunciation to Mary of the Incarnation of Christ, which has obvious Eucharistic significance. A painting portraying the Virgin's imminent but "good" death after an exemplary and worthy life would be, however, suitable for female congregations such as societies of Catholic lay sisters. Such sisterhoods provided many essential services to the Catholic community, caring for the poor, visiting the sick, catechizing children, cleaning and decorating the hidden churches, and singing at services. As unmarried women who took oaths of obedience and chastity, they would have looked to the Virgin Mary as a role model.[3]

Bor was a remarkable artist, born into a prominent and well-connected wealthy Catholic family – and later marrying into another – who did not, presumably, rely upon the sale of his paintings for a living. The preponderance of obscure subjects in his small output reflects the interests of an intellectual unconstrained by conventional taste. A voyage to Italy at age twenty-two, where he stayed in Rome and studied the works of Caravaggio and his followers, clearly affected his style. Bor's cool light, elegant rhythms, and luminous fabrics share many affinities with Orazio Gentileschi and the Utrecht Caravaggisti. Bor was a founding member of a society of Netherlandish artists in Rome, called the *Bentvueghels* (birds of a feather). In 1626 he returned to The Netherlands and settled in his hometown of Amersfoort, cultivating an elite circle of patrons, including Prince Frederick Henry of Orange-Nassau. In 1638, along with Jacob van Campen and a team of artists, Bor painted the decorations for one of the prince's hunting palaces (since destroyed).

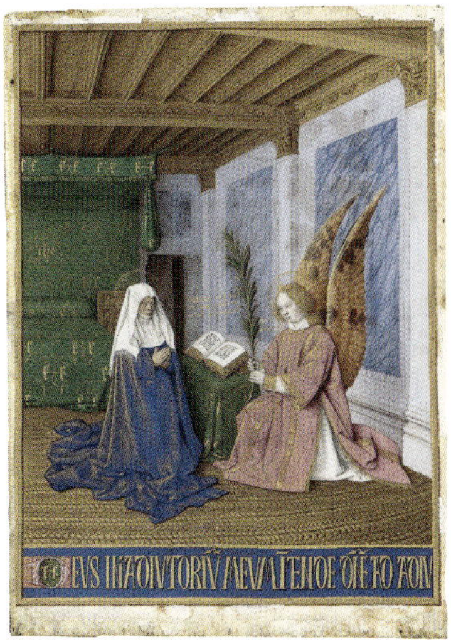

Jean Fouquet, *The Annunciation of the Virgin's Death*, from *The Book of Hours of Étienne Chevalier*, c. 1453–60, body colour on parchment. Musée Condé, Chantilly. Photo: Réunion des Musées Nationaux / Art Resource, NY

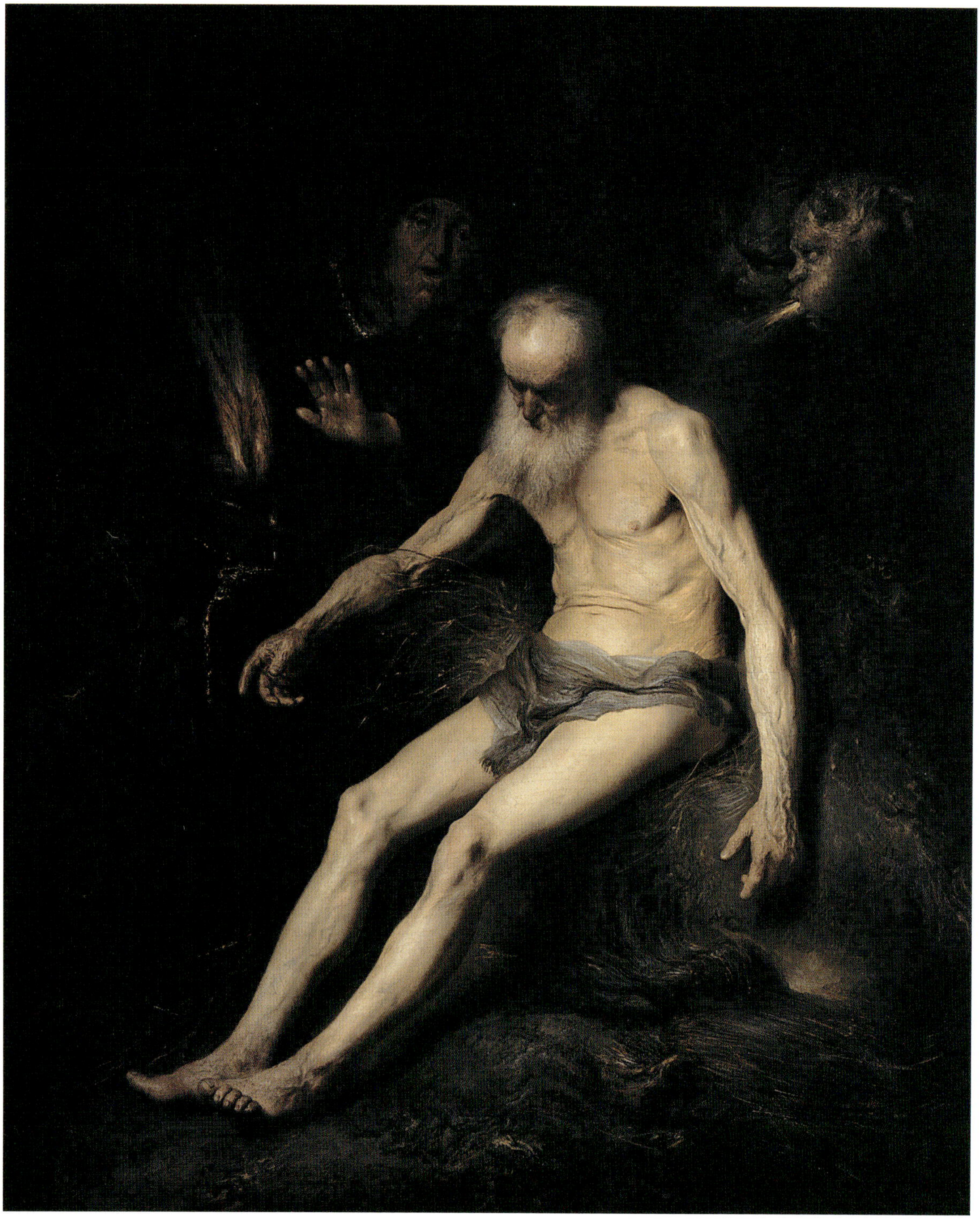

Jan Lievens (Dutch, 1607–1674), *Job*, 1631, oil on canvas, 171.5 × 148.6 cm. Gift of the National Art-Collections Fund of Great Britain, 1933 (4093)

JAN LIEVENS Job

Jan Lievens was a gifted painter, draughtsman, and printmaker. His talent, at least during his early years, rivalled that of Rembrandt, with whom he worked closely in Leiden from about 1625 to 1631. *Job* is regarded as one of Lievens' masterpieces.

The Old Testament Book of Job recounts the afflictions of a prosperous and devout man, who in the face of terrible misfortune refused to abandon his faith. Job's ordeals came through no fault of his own, but were the result of an argument between God and Satan. Job's faith had remained steadfast in times of wealth and good fortune, but Satan wanted to prove that it was not strong enough to withstand calamitous adversity. They agreed that Satan should put Job to the test. In various onslaughts, Job's livestock were stolen or slaughtered and his servants slain; and a hurricane razed the house where his sons and daughters were gathered and killed them. Finally, he was stricken with boils from head to foot. Job grieved as his world collapsed around him, yet refused to give in and forsake his God. His wife did not understand his tenacity, and scorned him for believing in such a cruel and unjust deity, urging him to "curse God and die!" Then three friends, who believed the misfortunes must be retribution for evil-doing, urged Job to confess and repent. But Job denied that he had sinned, and stayed resolute in his trust in God, thus defeating Satan. In the end Job's faith was justified as his health, prosperity, and family were all restored.

Lievens' painting of Job's grief is powerful. Job, in his state of deepest misery, is seated on a dung heap, as it is described in the Septuagint and Vulgate versions of the Bible (in modern translations it is less eloquently described as a mound of ashes). The canvas is large, and Job's elderly and emaciated life-size body fills most of it, lit in a strong raking light from the left that puts all else in shadow. Out of the darkness loom two frightful evil spirits breathing smoke and fire, and the grimacing face of Job's wife, admonishing him. It is also just possible to make out Job's richly jewelled clothes – the feathered plume of his hat is often mistaken for a torch flame – lying next to him, a reminder of all that he has lost. Lievens has omitted the detail of Job's affliction with boils, and does not include any narrative scenes showing the destruction wrought upon Job's family and possessions. By focusing instead on his subject's haggard features and aged, skeletal, anguished form, Lievens tells us all there is to know about Job's spirits, and suggests a quality of Christ-like solitude in his suffering.

The works painted by Lievens and Rembrandt during their time together in Leiden are often difficult to tell apart, revealing that the two must have had some kind of mutually inspiring artistic friendship. They both favoured using strong chiaroscuro effects from artificial sources, and both began experimenting with impasto. They also, on occasion, used the same models and borrowed each other's compositions. There is little evidence that they ever shared a studio, however, as has been suggested in the past. The two did not live far from each other, and probably had studios in their homes like most other artists in seventeenth-century Holland. Rembrandt, often considered one of the world's greatest artists, is much better known today than Lievens, but at this early stage in their careers it is Lievens who appears to have been the driving force of the two. Lievens painted *Job* a year or so before Rembrandt painted *A Woman at Her Toilet* (see p. 16).[1] They are both astounding pieces, but *Job* is larger and more monumental than anything Rembrandt had yet to produce, including *A Woman*, and Lievens' use of impasto to vividly describe Job's sagging and aging flesh is far more assertive than Rembrandt's loose brushstrokes in the sleeves of his central figure.

In 1632 Lievens moved to England and then finally settled in Amsterdam. Although much of his later painted work does not live up to the heights he achieved in *Job*, his drawings include some of the finest examples of Dutch portraiture and landscape in the medium.

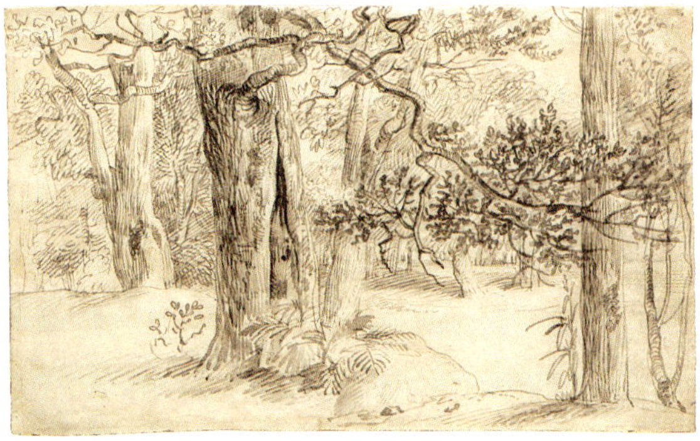

Jan Lievens, *Woodland Interior*, c. 1655–65, pen and brown ink on Japan paper, 22.8 × 37.8 cm. Purchased 1949 (5063)

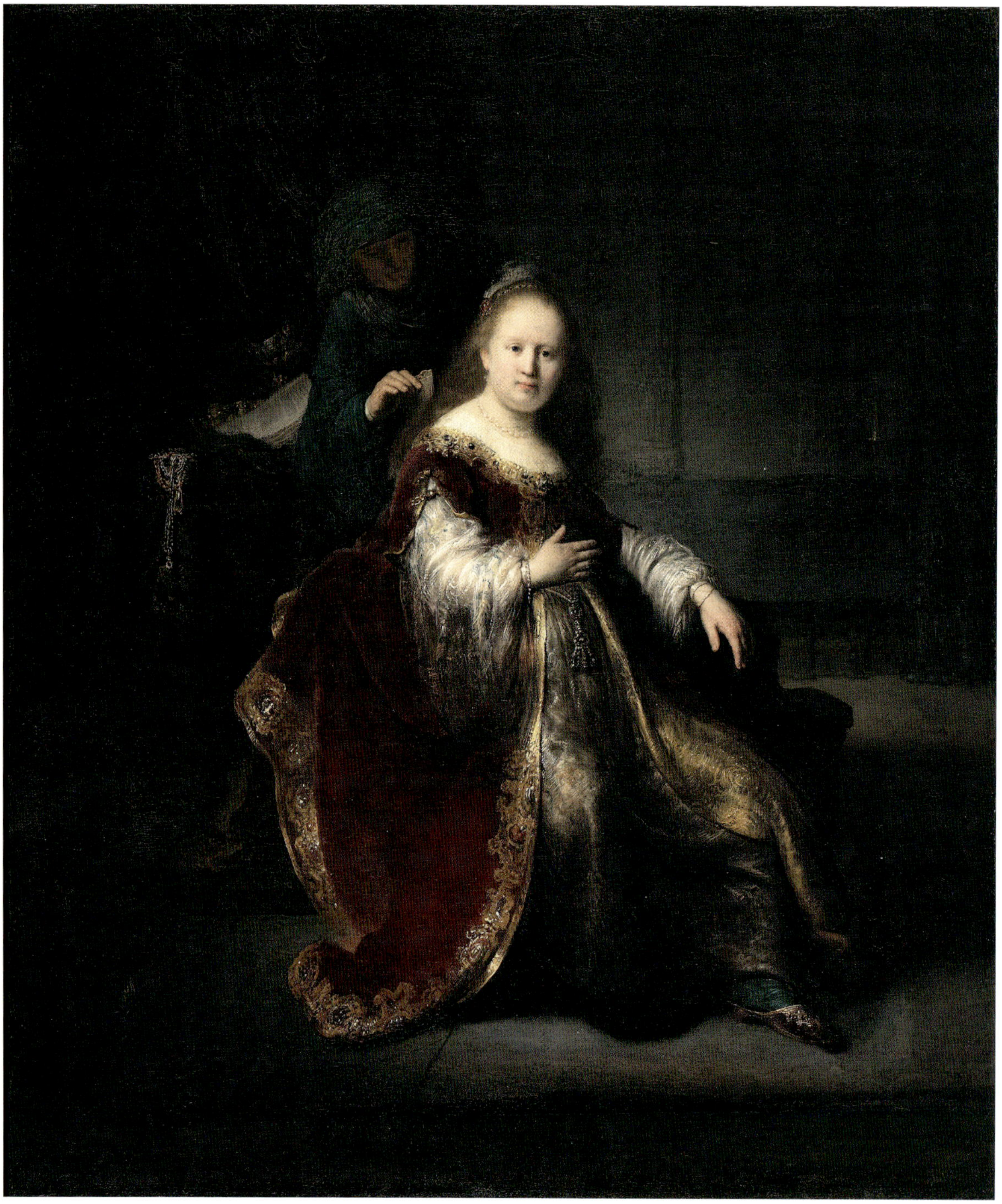

Rembrandt van Rijn (Dutch, 1606–1669), *A Woman at Her Toilet*, 1632 or 1633, oil on linen, 109.2 × 94.4 cm. Purchased 1953 (6089)

Rembrandt made this painting around age twenty-six shortly after leaving Leiden in 1631 for the busy cosmopolitan centre of Amsterdam. During his first years there, he worked for the art dealer Hendrik van Uylenburgh and lived in his house, where he probably met van Uylenburg's niece Saskia, whom he married in 1634.

In Leiden, Rembrandt had begun painting compositions with single figures, dramatic lighting, and a narrow tonal range of rich colours. He honed his mature style in Amsterdam, introducing such new techniques as the looser, more expressive brushstroke in the woman's clothing, the relatively large representation (half life-size) of a figure shown full-length, and the use of canvas as a support (this is one of his earliest canvases).

But who is Rembrandt's beautiful woman? In the eighteenth century, the painting was rather cryptically called *The Jewish Bride*, probably because of the subject's exotic costume and the bedroom setting. Nineteenth-century specialists were bent on recognizing various members of the artist's family, particularly his wife, Saskia, or his sister Liesbeth.[1]

Although today many still favour Saskia, naming any unspecified sitter is highly subjective, even with securely documented portraits for comparison, such as the drawing on which Rembrandt wrote: "This is my wife, made when she was 21 years old, three days after our betrothal on 8 June 1633." With this drawing, Saskia has been convincingly identified in some Rembrandt works, but the woman's countenance in the Ottawa painting is, to my mind, only vaguely reminiscent of Saskia's facial type.[2]

Twentieth-century scholars have preferred to see heroines from the Old Testament in the image. The painting entered the collection in 1953 as *The Toilet of Bathsheba*, but it lacks any identifying attribute, such as the letter Bathsheba received from King David, or David himself watching nearby. Some scholars claim the scene represents Esther dressing for her meeting with Ahasuerus, whom she would convince to stop the massacre of the Jews.[3] Esther, a saviour of her people, was revered by the seventeenth-century Dutch, who drew parallels to their own struggle to escape Spanish rule. Others argue for Judith, another saviour of her people.[4] But Judith adorning herself before seducing and then beheading Holofernes is usually shown in her tent near the enemy encampment.

From another angle, *A Woman at Her Toilet* invites a secular as much as a biblical reading: the contrast of youth and age could be meant to evoke *vanitas* (the fleeting aspects of mortality). Or, the composition may allude to Venus at her toilet. In the end, the dearth of attributes makes it impossible to establish the subject of this painting beyond doubt.

Rembrandt made several ambiguous paintings. *A Woman Bathing*, for example, has been variously identified as Susanna, Bathsheba, the goddess Diana, the nymph Callisto, or Rembrandt's mistress – or even a "mulier impudica," a familiar image of immodesty at the time.[5] The many interpretations generated by such works reveal the power of Rembrandt's artistry: his skill at suggesting that there is a story, while leaving it to us to imagine what it might be.

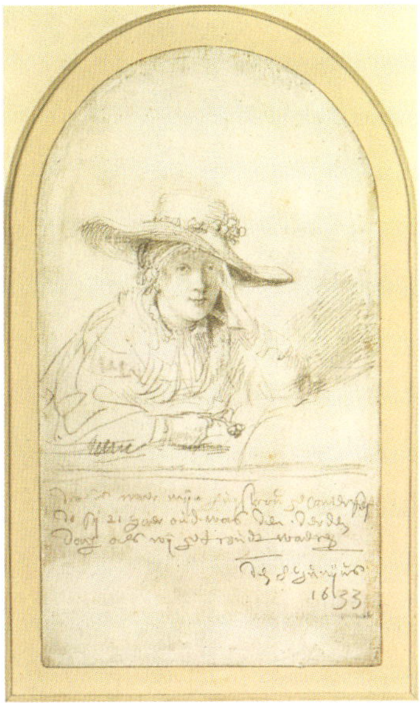

Rembrandt van Rijn, *Portrait of Saskia*, 1633, silverpoint on vellum, 18.5 × 10.7 cm. Staatliche Museen zu Berlin, Kupferstichkabinett, Berlin (KdZ 1152). Photo: Bildarchiv Preussischer Kulturbesitz / Art Resource, NY

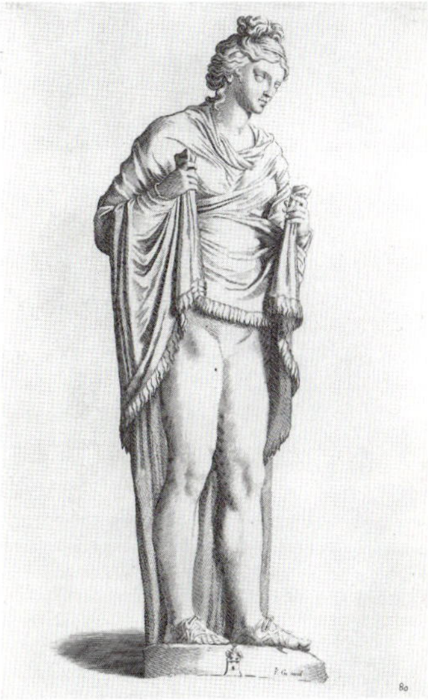

Giovanni Frederico Greuter, *Mulier Impudica* c. 1640, engraving, 36.9 × 23.2 cm. Rijksmuseum, Amsterdam

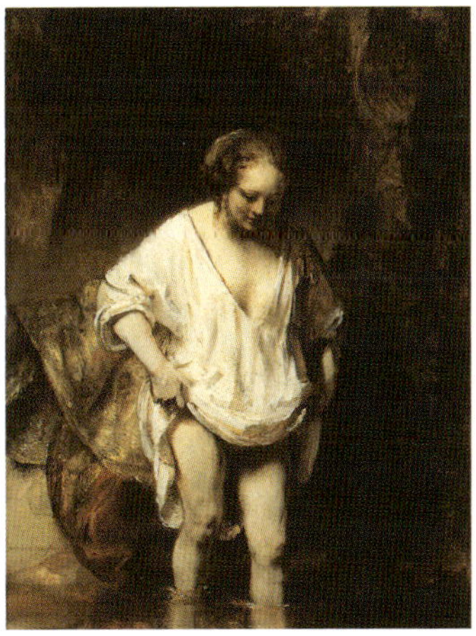

Rembrandt van Rijn, *A Woman Bathing*, signed and dated 1654, oil on panel, 61.8 × 47 cm. National Gallery, London (NG54)

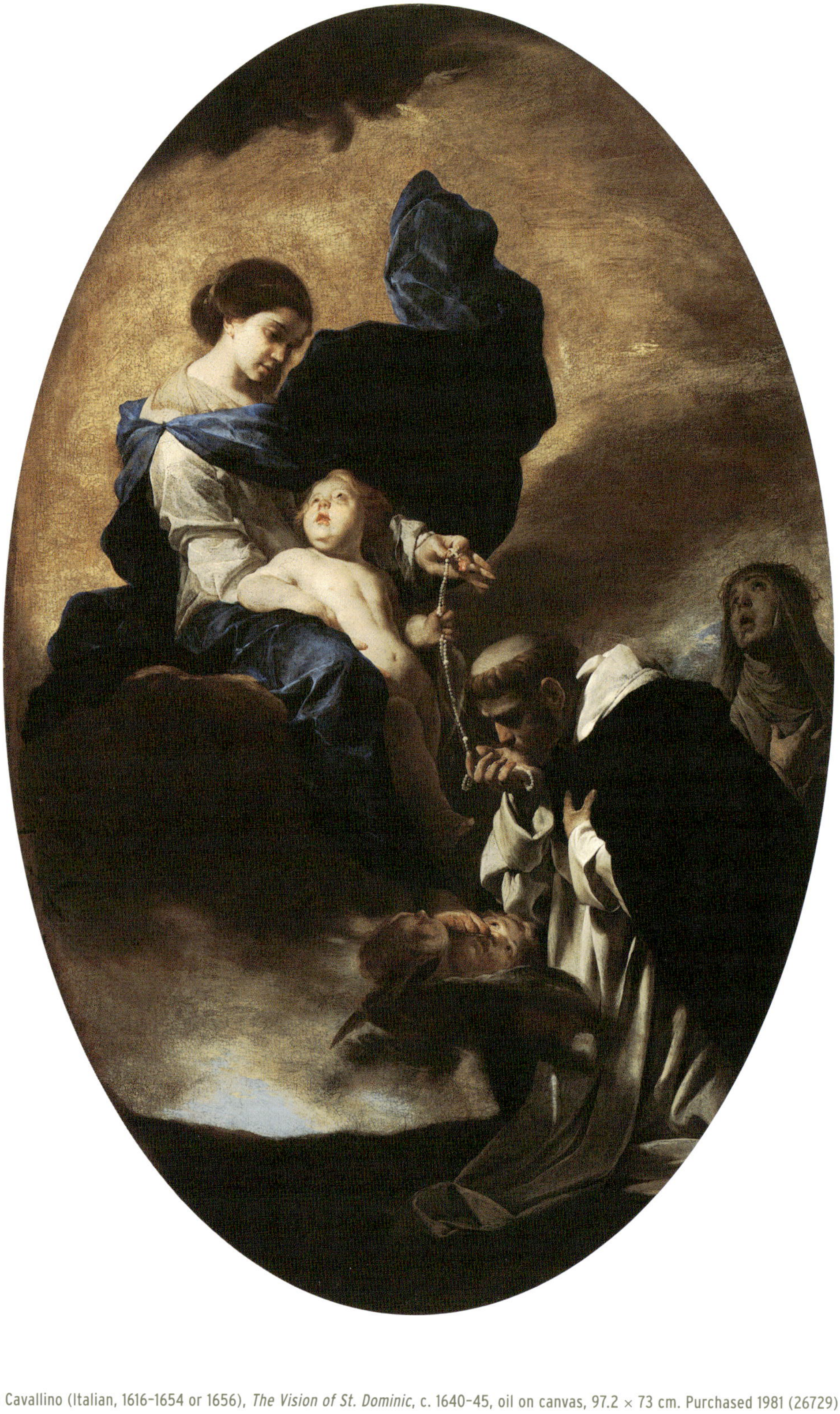

Bernardo Cavallino (Italian, 1616–1654 or 1656), *The Vision of St. Dominic*, c. 1640–45, oil on canvas, 97.2 × 73 cm. Purchased 1981 (26729)

Bernardo Cavallino was a gifted and original artist working in Naples during the first half of the seventeenth century. The quality and number of his extant paintings – some eighty autograph works[1] – indicate a successful, if rather short career. We know little about his life, except that he probably died around age forty.[2] The lack of documentary evidence stems partially from the fact that he painted few public commissions and apparently no large-scale decorations for the church or nobility. Most of his works are small paintings made for private collectors, similar in scale and subject to *The Vision of St. Dominic*. Because these were mainly in private hands (and now widely dispersed), Cavallino was largely forgotten after his death, only to be rediscovered in the twentieth century. However, Bernardo de Dominici, an eighteenth-century Neapolitan art historian, placed Cavallino among a handful of important painters from Naples, calling him the Poussin of the Neapolitans, and describing his style as a mixture of Guido Reni, Rubens, and Titian.[3]

This lovely painting illustrates Cavallino's ability to combine a compelling naturalism in his figures with a vibrant palette and delicate brushwork. The result is a sensitive portrayal of tender emotion. The humble beauty of the Virgin's face reveals the influence of Caravaggio's practice of using common people drawn from life as his models, but Cavallino has softened her features and given her a quality of gentle tranquillity reminiscent of Velázquez's *The Needlewoman*.[4] The lively blue of Mary's mantle and the way it billows energetically around her brings to mind the bright palette and flowing draperies in the late works of Jusepe de Ribera (d. 1652), who was then the leading Neapolitan painter.

That Cavallino's oeuvre shows a broad spectrum of influences was a natural consequence of life in a cosmopolitan city. Capital of the Spanish kingdoms of Naples and Sicily – all of southern Italy – Naples was three times larger than Rome, and the next largest city in Europe after London and Paris. Caravaggio's innovations were absorbed very quickly by Neapolitan painters when he visited in 1606–07 and again in 1609–10. Aspects of Bolognese classicism arrived in 1612 and 1621 with Guido Reni and in 1630–31 with Domenichino. In addition, the works of Poussin, van Dyck, and Rubens could all be found in important art collections.

Judging by its size and subject, *St. Dominic* was meant for private devotion. The painting depicts the saint's vision of the Virgin offering him a string of rosary beads. Tradition credits St. Dominic with instituting the devotion of the rosary: a sequence of prayers dedicated to Mary and recited using a string of beads to count repetitions. St. Dominic (1170–1221) was one of many saints whose veneration was fostered during the Counter-Reformation, particularly in the Spanish realms, due to his life-long battle against heresy – a cause important to the Spanish monarchy since the fifteenth century, when Queen Isabel and King Ferdinand expelled the last Muslims from Spain.

In the painting, Dominic wears a black hooded cloak over a white tunic and scapular, which is the habit of the Order of Black Friars (or Dominicans) that he founded. He is often shown with other saints of his order – here, Catherine of Siena – and with a lily, the symbol of chastity, which we see on the ground before him. Cavallino expertly conveys Dominic's humble gratitude by the simple gesture of his left hand held over his heart, and the delicate grasp of his fingers as he holds the rosary and kisses it. The recitation of the rosary is a private act; one can easily imagine how Cavallino's small but eloquent painting would have aided the imagination of a worshipper.

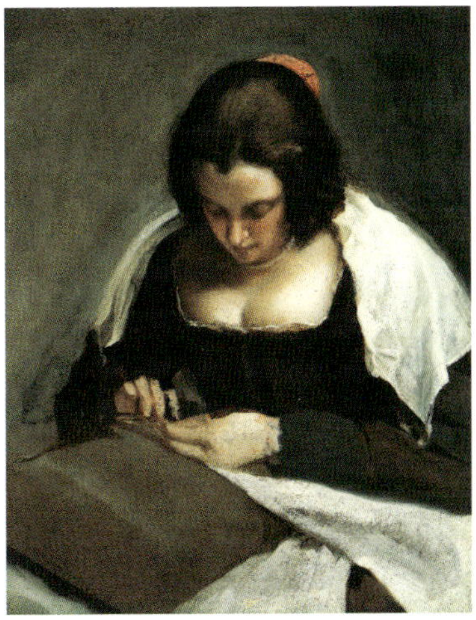

Diego Velázquez, *The Needlewoman*, c. 1640/50, oil on canvas, 740 × 600 cm. Andrew W. Mellon Collection, The National Gallery of Art, Washington, D.C. (1937.1.81)

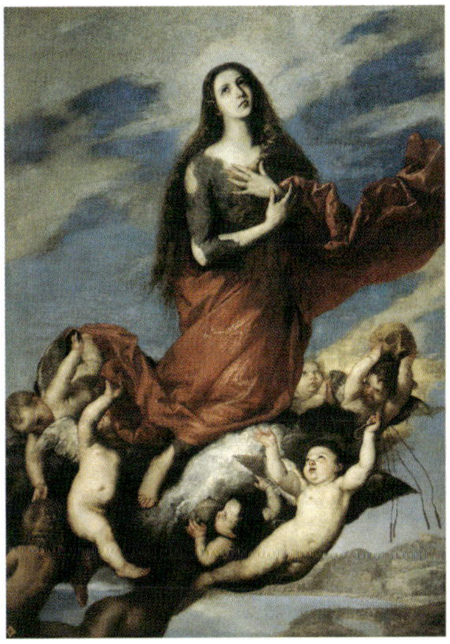

Jusepe de Ribera, *The Assumption of the Magdalen*, 1636, oil on canvas, 256 × 193 cm. Real Academia de Bellas Artes de San Fernando, Madrid (636)

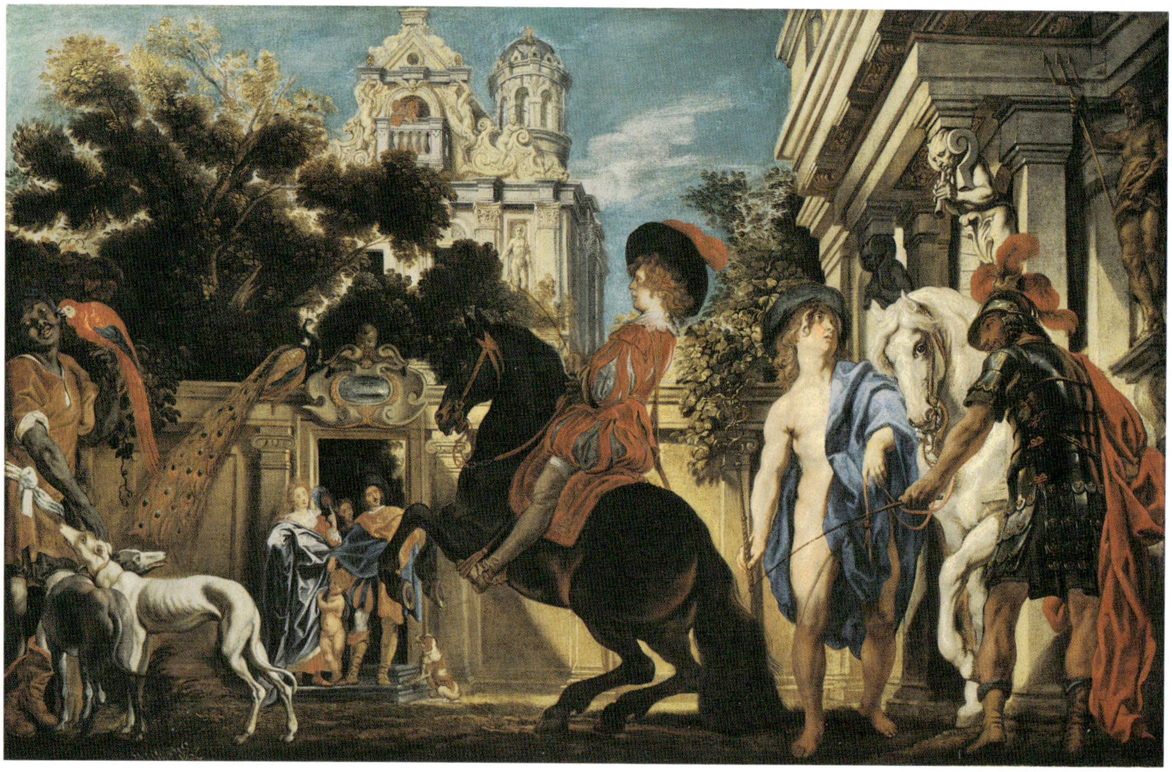

Jacob Jordaens (Flemish, 1593–1678), *A Young Cavalier Executing a Levade in the Presence of Mars and Mercury*, c. 1645, oil on canvas, 96 × 153 cm.
Purchased 1965 (14810)

JACOB JORDAENS A Young Cavalier Executing a Levade in the Presence of Mars and Mercury

> May Pallas Athena be your guide, Cupid your page, Mars the captain who directs your courage; may your own mount be the winged Pegasus, and may Mercury as lackey be ever at your side.
>
> – *inscription on a print of Charles II on horseback*[1]

This lively and colourful painting is a *modello* for a tapestry, one of a series of eight on the theme of horsemanship. A complete cycle, sometimes called the *Riding School*, is in Vienna, and three other models for the series are known.[2] Much smaller than the woven tapestry, which is some four by five metres, the *modello* functioned as a handy tool for the artist or dealer to show prospective buyers the appearance of the finished work.

Jordaens, a foremost painter of the Flemish Baroque, was highly regarded during his lifetime. Since then, he has been overshadowed by the more glamorous Rubens and van Dyck, who were painters to the princes of Europe. Jordaens spent his life in his native city of Antwerp, working primarily for the bourgeoisie and clergy. Tapestries formed a significant part of his production, and after Rubens died in 1640, Jordaens became Antwerp's pre-eminent tapestry designer, making at least seven series on historical and contemporary subjects.

The *Riding School* comprises six scenes showing riders executing traditional figures of *haute école* dressage, including the levade seen here, plus *The Creation of the Horse*, and the *Presentation of the Horses*. In this most formal kind of training, the horse responds to barely perceptible signals with precision movements.[3] For the levade, he must bend his haunches deeply, lift his body no more than 45 degrees, tuck in his forelegs, and hold his head straight and close to his body, maintaining the position for as long as strength and skill allow (usually no more than five seconds). It seems effortless but is exceedingly demanding for both horse and rider.

The scenes designed by Jordaens depend upon engravings by Crispijn de Passe II (1597–1670) in *Le Maneige Royal*, the most important seventeenth-century treatise on haute-école riding forms, published for Louis XIII of France.[4] De Passe's prints influenced equestrian portraiture throughout Europe, notably in paintings by Velázquez, Rubens, and van Dyck. The prints were didactic in purpose, illustrating the riding positions in great detail. For his tapestries, Jordaens added allegorical and genre elements. Here, Mars points a crop at the rider's sorrel horse, while Mercury holds the reins of a riderless grey. Their presence is explained by the astrological belief that planets govern the appearance and character of animals as well as people, from Pasquale Caracciolo's *La Gloria del cavallo* (Venice 1566). He associated Mars with reddish-brown horses – sorrels and bays – who were choleric, proud, and restless, and Mercury with all other horses – from white to black to piebald – who were spirited and courageous.[5] Mercury, the messenger god, guide, and teacher, and Mars, the god of war, decisive and strong, make excellent grooms to the able rider, who commands the strength and energy of a spirited stallion. Neptune, the god whom the Ancients thought created the horse, presides as a sculpture from the building behind.

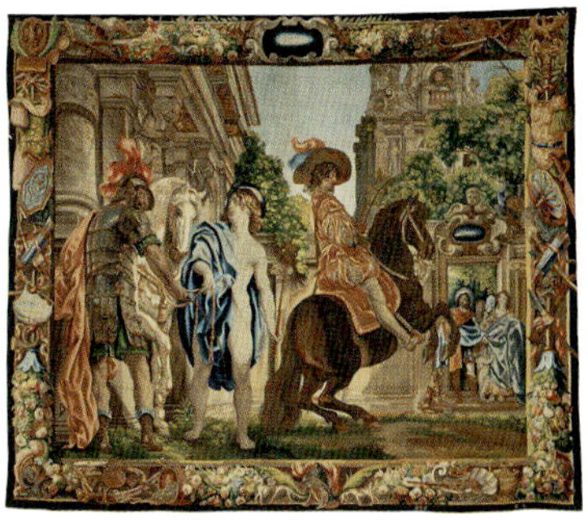

Young Cavalier Executing a Levade in the Presence of Mercury and Mars, tapestry woven by Everard Leyniers after Jordaens, by 1666, 410 × 598 cm. Vienna, Kunsthistorisches Museum

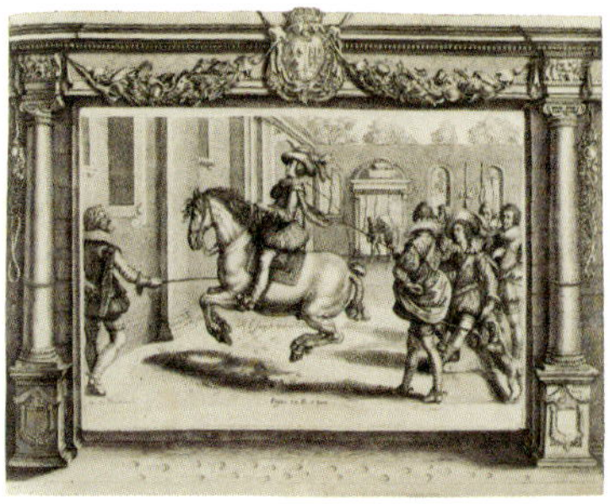

Crispijn de Passe II, from *Le Maneige Royal*, by Antoine Pluvinel, 1632, engraving. Universiteitsbibliotheek, Amsterdam

Our museums are filled today with paintings not tapestries, so it is hard to realize that tapestries were much more valued in their day. They played an important role in the art, propaganda, and liturgy of European courts and churches from the late medieval period onwards. Because they were extremely expensive to make, tapestries became associated with the aristocracy, who could afford them, and had rooms large enough to hang them. As well as providing insulation for draughty castles and villas, tapestries offered opportunities for discreet boasting by depicting scenes of virtue, skill, and heroism, meant to reflect on their owner's character and achievements. Jordaens' series of tapestries on horsemanship would have been an apt choice for any aristocrat.

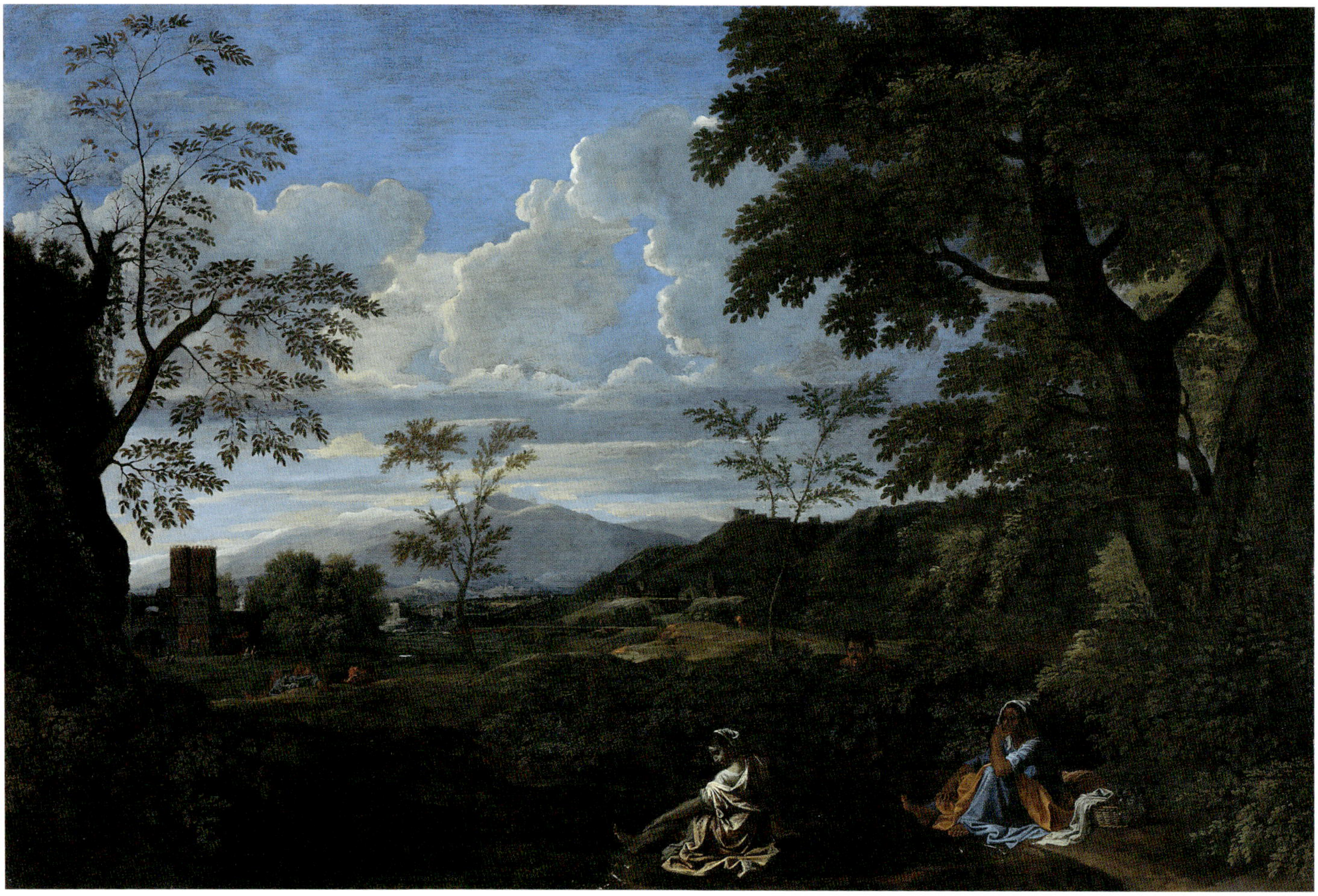

Nicolas Poussin (French, 1594–1665), *Landscape with a Woman Washing Her Feet* 1650, oil on canvas, 116.5 × 174.7 cm. Gift of H.S. Southam, Ottawa, 1944 (4587)

If Poussin had a particular story in mind when he painted this tranquil scene set somewhere outside Rome, it is long forgotten. Just sixteen years later, the art historian Félibien, who knew Poussin well, simply described it as a landscape with a woman washing her feet.[1]

Born in France, Poussin spent almost his entire career in Rome, painting for private collectors rather than for the large-scale church and palace commissions that occupied his contemporaries. Similar in size to this painting, his works fit well into middle- or upper-class homes. Many of his clients shared Poussin's interest in ancient mythology and history, especially in his later works, where he explored the great moral dilemmas (usually involving the triumph of will over passion) faced by heroes found in the writings of Stoic historians, then in vogue among his French patrons.

Poussin often illustrated arcane and even unknown stories, and only a handful of his landscapes have descriptive titles that do not refer to a particular literary source. His figures always add to the emotional content: the exact subject of *Landscape with a Man Killed by a Snake* is unknown, but most agree it reverberates with the victim's horror and fear, as if the scene were devised solely to explore those emotions.[2] The figures in his paintings are never mere staffage,[3] as in the work of his contemporary Claude Lorrain.

Altogether, it seems unlikely that Poussin had no story in mind when he picked up his brush to paint this bucolic image. Even if we cannot identify the narrative, we can sense the peaceful mood that pervades the scene. Some people soak up the sun while others go calmly about their activities. In the foreground, a young woman dips her foot in the water. Her companion rests in a pose of quiet introspection, perhaps even sadness. The only minor disruption – seen by the viewer alone – is the satyr peeping over the hedge.

Many subjects have been suggested for this painting, but none completely convince. A recent proposal is the myth of Vertumnus and Pomona.[4] After many unsuccessful attempts, Vertumnus disguises himself as an old woman and tries to woo the goddess of gardens and orchards by convincing her of his virtues – failing until he reveals himself in his own youthful body, and Pomona is smitten. The older "woman" in the painting does indeed appear to be a man – notice the dark skin, large foot and hands, muscular forearms, and pronounced wrist-bone – but why is the satyr there? And why does Vertumnus sit so far from Pomona, staring blankly at her back instead of pleading his case?

The story of Hercules and Omphale better fits the mood of Poussin's quiet landscape, and explains the satyr. Hercules was sold as a slave to Omphale, queen of Lydia (present-day Turkey), because he killed the young man Iphitus in a fit of madness. Ovid recounts how the satyr Pan spied Omphale walking with Hercules, and fell in love with her. Ovid also describes Omphale dressing Hercules in her own clothes:

> She gave him gauzy tunics in Gaetulian purple dipped; she gave him the dainty girdle, which but now girt her waist. For his belly the girdle was too small; he undid the clasps of the tunics to thrust out his big hands. The bracelets he had broken, not made to fit those arms; his big feet split the little shoes.[5]

Hercules felt deeply dishonoured by his slavery, and dressing as a woman compounded his shame. Poussin has represented the hero in a pose that would have been immediately recognizable to his contemporaries as that of Melancholia, widely known through Dürer's famous engraving.

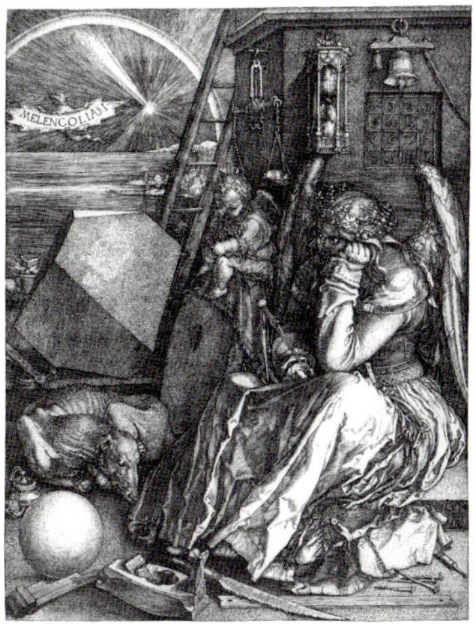

Albrecht Dürer, *Melancholia I*, 1514, engraving, 24.1 × 19.2 cm. British Museum, London

Of all the subjects suggested over the years, Hercules's enslavement to Omphale accords best with Poussin's interest in Stoic philosophy. Hercules was a favourite hero of the Stoics because his dual nature – half human, half god – frequently led him down the wrong path, and made his choices between virtue and vice difficult. Furthermore, Poussin's idyllic landscape matches Plutarch's description of Lydia as a land of peace and security during the years of Hercules' servitude.

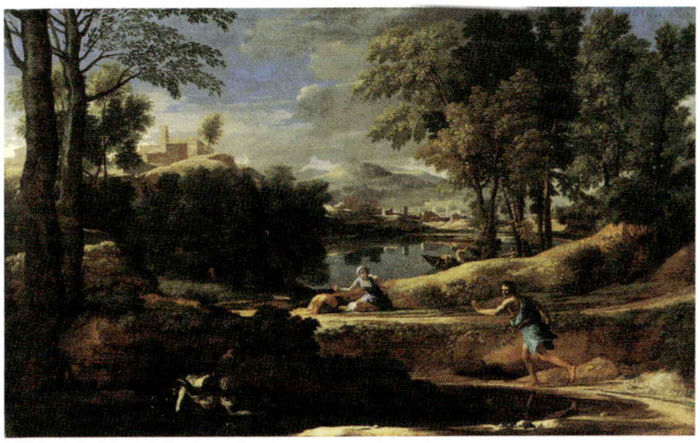

Nicolas Poussin, *Landscape with a Man Killed by a Snake*, 1648, oil on canvas, 119.4 × 198.8 cm. National Gallery, London (NG 5763)

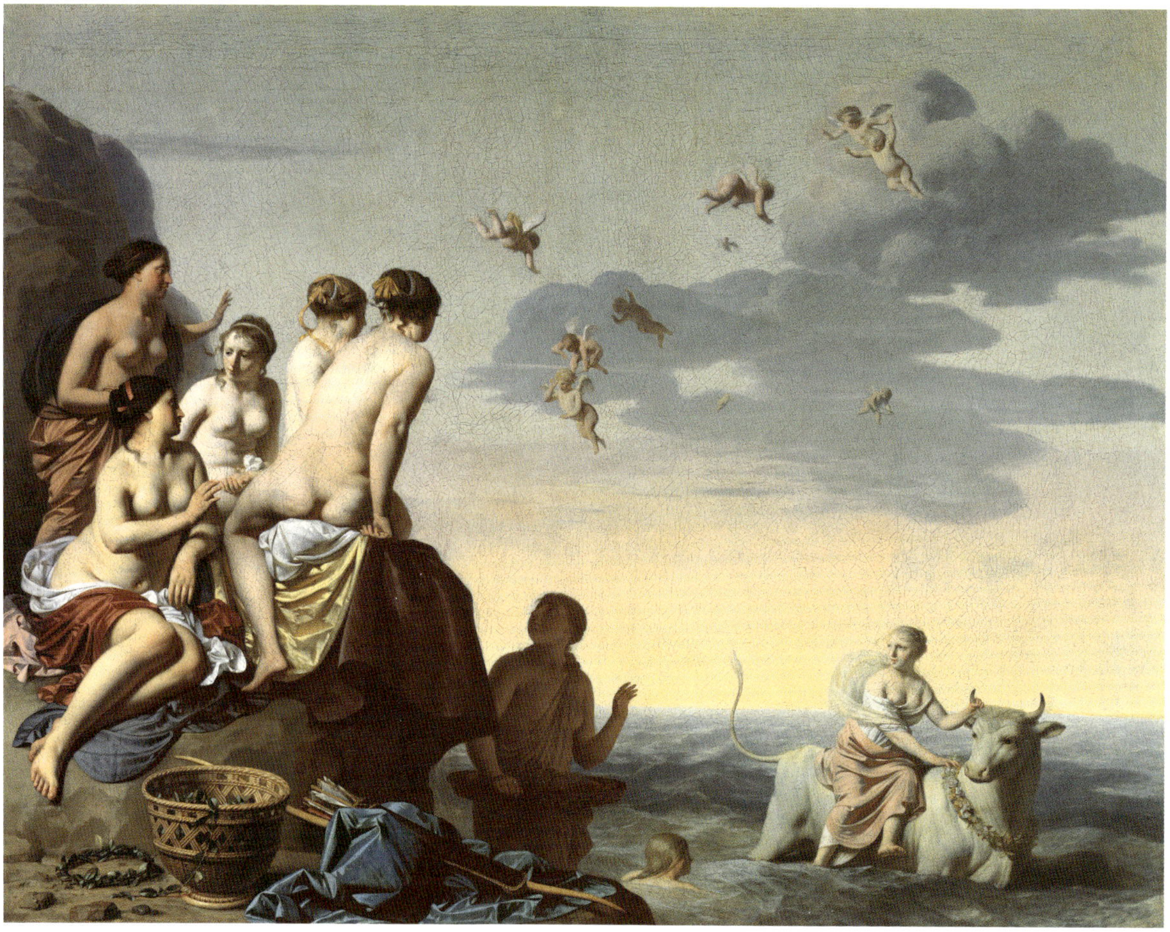

Caesar Boetius van Everdingen (Dutch, c. 1617–1678), *The Rape of Europa*, c. 1650, oil on canvas, 118.1 × 151.1 cm. Gift of Federal Construction Inc., Montreal, 1998 (39830)

Van Everdingen's paintings, so crisp, clearly delineated, evenly lit, and idealized, and usually of classical subjects like *The Rape of Europa*, do not fit popular notions of Dutch art, which we tend to associate with the naturalistic interiors of Vermeer and Pieter de Hooch, the gritty tavern scenes of Jan Steen, the lively portraits of Frans Hals, or the psychologically penetrating works of Rembrandt. Nevertheless, the art of the "Haarlem Classicists" (or history painters) was a fashionable alternative in centres like The Hague and Haarlem that has been unfairly overshadowed in the history books by styles deemed more indigenously Dutch.

Classical painting was particularly fostered at the court of Stadholder Frederick Henry, Prince of Orange, and his wife, Amalia von Solms.[1] The classical taste spread quickly amongst the gentry and wealthy bourgeoisie, and a viable market for paintings like *The Rape of Europa* made it possible for van Everdingen to enjoy a successful career as a history painter specializing in mythological and allegorical subjects. He spent most of his career in his native town of Alkmaar, but also worked in Haarlem and The Hague, where he collaborated with Jacob van Campen, Holland's pre-eminent classical architect, on several projects. These included the Oranjezaal – the central hall dedicated to Frederick Henry's heroic deeds and the propagation of the dynastic claims of the Orange-Nassau family – in the newly erected royal palace at Huis ten Bosch in 1648.

The classical world, rediscovered in the Renaissance, continued to interest seventeenth-century artists and their patrons. Study by classical scholars and the formation of great collections by connoisseurs had brought the knowledge of ancient art and architecture to a wide public. The loves of the ancient gods, especially of Jupiter for Europa, were extremely popular subjects for art throughout Europe, not only because of their classical sources, but because they gave such a delightful excuse to paint and display female nudes. According to Ovid,[2] Europa, the daughter of the King of Tyre, was spotted by Zeus as she was playing on the seashore with her attendants. He fell in love and set about abducting her. To do this, he approached her in the guise of a white bull from a herd grazing nearby. At first frightened, Europa gradually lost her fear of the large beast, stroking his flanks and placing a garland around his horns. At last, she sat innocently upon his back, whereupon Jupiter immediately swam out to sea, taking Europa to the island of Crete, where he returned to his normal form and ravished her.

The pose of the maiden sitting on the rocks with her back to the viewer is based on one of the Three Graces from a fresco on the ceiling of the Farnesina palace painted by Raphael and assistants between 1517 and 1519. It is not a direct copy, since van Everdingen has changed the position of her arms, and painted her in reverse, but the source is clear. Although van Everdingen never travelled to Rome or saw the famous frescos himself, many Northern artists did, and brought back copies that he could easily have seen. He also may have referred to Raimondi's well-known engravings, in which the maiden is likewise reversed. As well, the pose was a favourite of the Utrecht artist Cornelis van Poelenburgh, who did go to Italy, and whose style influenced van Everdingen.

Despite the classical source and the Renaissance iconography, van Everdingen has added a few contemporary touches to this painting. The wicker basket seen in the left foreground resembles Brazilian and Guinean baskets documented by Dutch artists in the 1630s and 1640s during the Dutch mission in South America.[3] And the iridescent fabrics draping the plump maidens are the same as those seen in other portraits of well-dressed, wealthy Dutch ladies. Van Everdingen's sumptuous rendition of the maidens' clothing and contours suggests he meant to please the eye at least as much as the intellect.

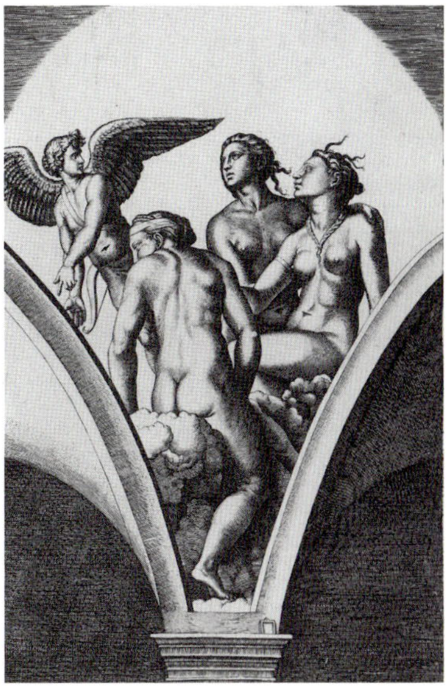

Marcantonio Raimondi after Raphael, *Cupid and the Three Graces* from the Villa Farnesina, 1517–19, engraving, 30.6 × 20.6 cm. The British Museum, London

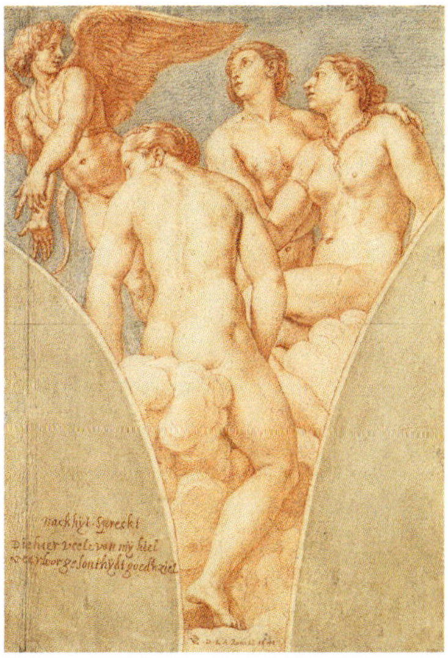

Pieter van Lint, *Cupid and the Three Graces* from the Villa Farnesina, 1641, red and black chalk with brown wash on laid paper, 40.9 × 28.6 cm. Private collection, Toronto. Photo: National Gallery of Canada

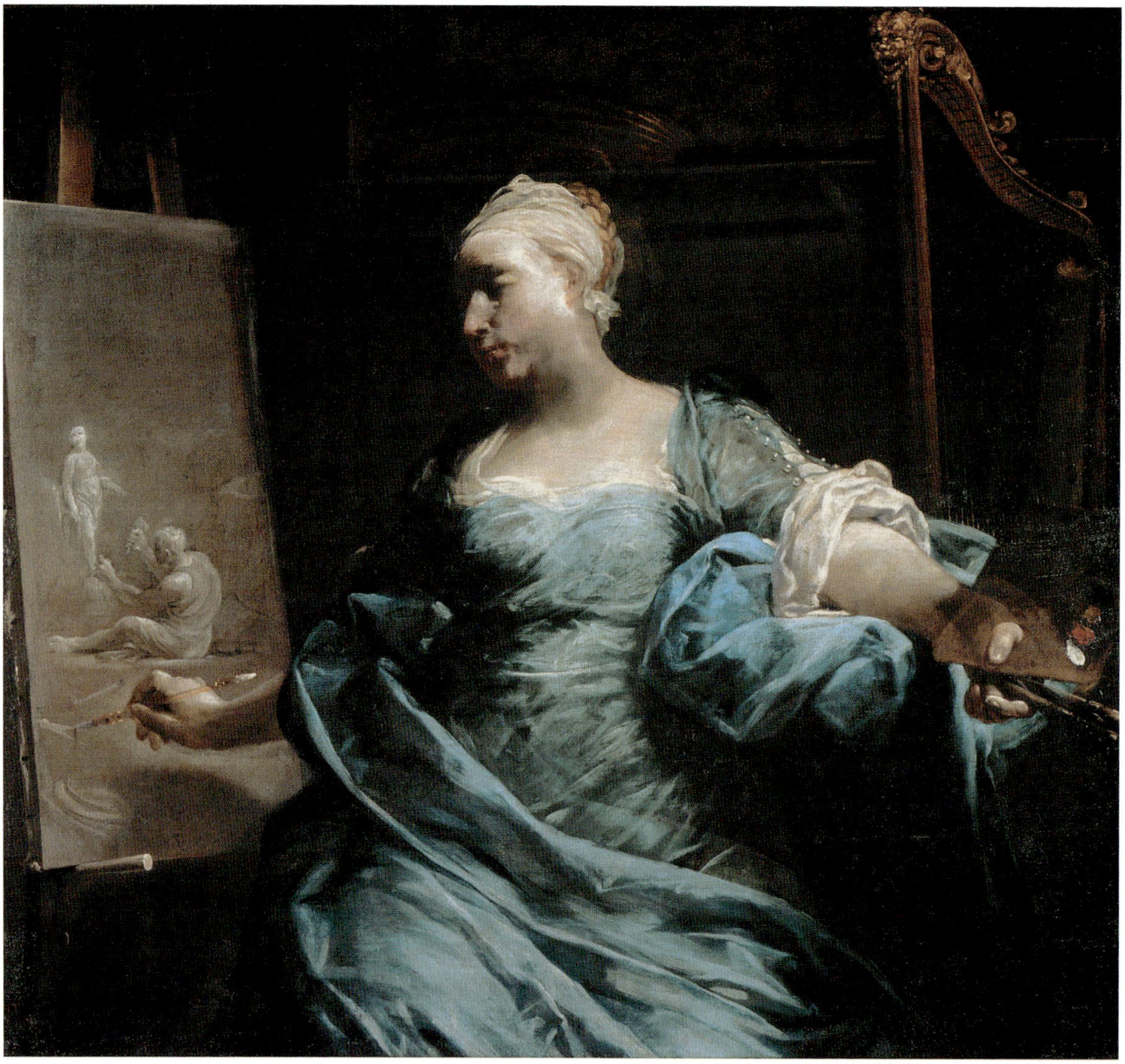

Giuseppe Maria Crespi (Italian, 1665–1747), *An Allegory of the Arts*, c. 1730, oil on canvas, 26.5 × 138.5 cm. Purchased 1996 (38019)

By the time Crespi made *An Allegory of the Arts*, the art of painting had been well-established – in Italy since the sixteenth century – as being a liberal art and not the manual labour of an artisan. The distinction was not inconsequential as the artist's place in society was at stake: should a painter be considered a craftsman, on a par with carpenters and masons, or an intellectual? Following a ranking first established in Antiquity, by the Middle Ages the seven liberal arts studied in the universities were usually considered to comprise grammar, rhetoric, logic, arithmetic, astronomy, geometry, and music (because of its mathematical sense of proportion and harmony). None of the plastic arts, such as painting or sculpture, were included on this list.[1] During the Renaissance, especially in Italy, voices were raised in protest against this position, Leonardo da Vinci the most outspoken among them. He and others argued that painting should be counted among the liberal arts because artists needed to know arithmetic and geometry to understand and use perspective; the latter was an important aspect of Renaissance painting. Even though the battle had long been won by the eighteenth century, the issue still remained a vital one to painters, who continued, somewhat defensively, to champion the inclusion of their art on the ancient list. Crespi's *An Allegory of the Arts* is an articulation of these abstract notions in pictorial form.

For his iconography, Crespi drew on Cesare Ripa's *Iconologia*, first published 1593, a popular reference manual to allegories and symbols, including codified ways of representing personifications of the arts. Ripa describes *Arte*, meaning the representational arts of painting and sculpture, as dressed in green and holding a brush and chisel. Crespi's personification has most of these attributes: she holds a painter's palette and brushes in her left hand; to her right stands an easel supporting a stretched canvas; and beneath her blue outer drapery she wears a greenish dress, as Ripa recommends. But Crespi has added further attributes for the disciplines of draughtsmanship (or *disegno*), architecture, sculpture, and music. In Arte's right hand is the draughtsman's *porte-crayon*, a device made to hold a piece of chalk; with it, she draws a compass, the attribute of architecture. On the canvas before her, she has painted a sculptor using a hammer and chisel to create the statue of a woman. And the harp and the lute (lying flat on the mantel above her head) behind her are both attributes of music.

Crespi was an original and innovative artist, in style and technique, as well as in the interpretations of the subjects he painted. By representing a sculptor on the stretched canvas, he not only alludes directly to the art of sculpture, but also to the myth of Pygmalion, an evocative metaphor for the creative process essential to all art forms, since the tale is literally a "creation myth," wherein the artist's work comes to life. According to Ovid,[2] the sculptor Pygmalion made a statue of a woman so perfect that he fell in love with his own art work, and prayed to Venus that he might be blessed with so beautiful a wife, whereupon the goddess brought the sculpture to life. Crespi has thus represented in pictorial form all of the aspects of his chosen profession: the practical side in the form of tools and musical instruments, the intellectual element through the drawing of the compass; and the creative facet through the painting of the sculptor.

Crespi spent most of his very successful career in his native Bologna, painting for the church and for private patrons, such as Prince Ferdinand de' Medici of Tuscany, who was particularly fond of genre scenes. Crespi also painted pastoral themes, still-lifes, and engaging informal portraits. In fact, radiography reveals that *An Allegory of the Arts* probably began its life as such a portrait. The earlier composition appears to be simply a woman in a languid, relaxed pose looking out toward the viewer, and includes no attributes of any kind. When Crespi finished his *Allegory*, the pigments he used would have been opaque and obscured all of the initial painting. However, some of the pigments have become transparent over time, and today some features of the original work are visible as shadows around the head and hand. These few *pentimenti* do not detract from Crespi's final conception of the Arts come to life in the shape of a beautiful woman with a vigorous and formidable presence.

NOTES

EL GRECO Saint Francis and Brother Leo Meditating on Death

1. David Davies, ed., *El Greco* (London: National Gallery Company, 2003), p. 61.
2. Émile Mâle, *L'Art religieux de la fin du XVIe siècle, du XVIIe siècle et du XVIIIe siècle* (Paris: A. Colin, 1951), pp. 206–16.
3. A version in Monforte de Lemos, Spain (Fundación de Nuestra Señora de la Antigua) is probably one of the first, having been documented as early as 1598; see José Álvarez Lopera, ed., *El Greco, Identity and Transformation* (Milan: Skira Editore, 1999), no. 36.
4. In 1913 a Spanish ophthalmologist put forward a famous but baseless notion that El Greco suffered from an extreme form of astigmatism: see Germán Beritens, *Aberraciones del Greco cientificamente consideradas* (Madrid, 1913).
5. Xavier de Salas and Fernando Marías, eds., *El Greco y el arte de su tiempo: las notas de El Greco a Vasari* (Madrid: Real Fundación de Toledo, 1992); and Fernándo Marías and Agustín Bustamante, eds., *La ideas artísticas de El Greco (Comentarios a un texto inédito)* (Madrid: Catédra, 1981).
6. One of the best of such studies is Jonathan Brown et al., eds., *El Greco of Toledo* (Boston: Little, Brown, and Company, 1982).

PETER PAUL RUBENS The Entombment

1. Originally quoted in Samuel van Hoogstraeten, *Inleyding tot de hooge schoole der Schilderkonst* (1678); English translation of citation from Jeffrey M. Muller, "Rubens's Theory and Practice of the Imitation of Art," *The Art Bulletin* 64, no. 2 (1982): 245.
2. He painted and drew several other depictions of the Entombment.
3. Muller, p. 239. For the inventory, see Jeffrey M. Muller, *Rubens: The Artist as Collector* (Princeton, New Jersey: Princeton University Press, 1989).

SIMON VOUET The Fortune-teller

1. For two excellent articles on gypsies and cardsharps in seventeenth-century painting, see Gail Feigenbaum, "Gamblers, Cheats, and Fortune-Tellers," in *Georges de La Tour and His World*, ed. Philip Conisbee (Washington: National Gallery of Art, 1996), pp. 149–81, and Helen Langdon, "Cardsharps, Gypsies, and Street Vendors," in *The Genius of Rome: 1592–1623*, ed. Beverly Louise Brown (London: Royal Academy of Arts, 2001), pp. 41–65, both of which were invaluable in the preparation of this entry.
2. Feigenbaum, p. 174.
3. Giovanni Antonio de' Pauli, *Le Barrarie del Mondo* [*sic*] (Bibliothèque nationale de France, c. 1590), repr. in Brown, *The Genius of Rome*, p. 46, fig. 12.
4. Founded in 1593, the Accademia di San Luca was one of the earliest European academies of art. (The Accademia di Disegno was established in Florence in 1563.)

PAULUS BOR The Annunciation of the Virgin's Death

1. Joachim Wolfgan von Moltke, "Die Gemälde des Paulus Bor von Amersfoort," *Westfalen: Hefte für Geschicte Kunst und Volkskunde* 55, nos. 1–2 (1977): 158–61.
2. *Dutch Classicism in Seventeenth-Century Painting* (Rotterdam: Museum Boijmans Van Beuningen and NAi Publishers, 1999), no. 20.
3. Benjamin J. Kaplan, "Confessionalism and Its Limits: Religion in Utrecht, 1600–1650," in *Masters of Light: Dutch Painters in Utrecht during the Golden Age*, ed. Joaneath A. Spicer and Lynn Federle Orr (New Haven and London: Yale University Press, 1997), p. 65. I would like to thank Dr. Xander van Eck for sharing insightful comments regarding the world of clandestine churches and societies of Catholic lay sisters in the Dutch Republic.

JAN LIEVENS Job

1. Rembrandt's painting is dated, but it is hard to make out whether it reads 1632 or 1633.

REMBRANDT VAN RIJN A Woman at Her Toilet

1. For a critique of identifying Rembrandt's sitters as family members, see Albert Blankert, "Looking at Rembrandt, Past and Present," in *Rembrandt: A Genius and His Impact*, ed. Albert Blankert (Melbourne and Sydney: National Gallery of Victoria and Art Exhibitions Australia Limited, 1997), especially pp. 42–49.
2. The Rembrandt Research Project does not describe her as Saskia, but mention of the same model appears in a number of other paintings from 1632. See J. Bruyn et al., *A Corpus of Rembrandt Paintings*, trans. D. Cook-Radmore, 3 vols. (The Hague, Dordrecht, Boston, and London: Stichting Foundation Rembrandt Research Project; M. Nijhoff Publishers, 1982–86), vol. 2, p. 272.
3. Madlyn Kahr made a strong case for Esther in her 1966 article "Rembrandt's Esther: A Painting and an Etching Newly Interpretated and Dated," *Oud-Holland* 81 (1966): 228–44.
4. Most notably the Rembrandt Research Project team; see Bruyn et al., *A Corpus of Rembrandt Paintings*, no. A64.
5. J. van der Waals, *De prentschat van Michiel Hinloopen: Een reconstructie van de eerste openbare papierkunstverzameling in Nederland* (Amsterdam: Rijksprentenkabinet, Rijksmuseum, 1988), p. 64, fig. 65, and p. 67, n. 113.

BERNARDO CAVALLINO The Vision of St. Dominic

1. Clovis Whitfield and Jane Martineau, eds., *Painting in Naples 1606–1705, from Caravaggio to Giordano* (London: Royal Academy of Arts and Weidenfeld and Nicolson, 1982), p. 135.
2. He may have died in the plague of 1656, or in 1654, as Bernardo de Dominici claimed.
3. Bernardo de Dominici, *Vite de' pittori, scultori, ed architetti*

napoletani, 3 vols. (Naples: Ricciardo, 1742–43, reprinted 1971 by Forni Editore, Bologna), vol. 3, p. 42.
4. Velázquez made two trips to Italy, in 1629–31 and 1649–51, and on both occasions he visited Naples.

JACOB JORDAENS A Young Cavalier Executing a Levade

1. The original reads: "Que Pallas soit vôtre guide, Cupidon vôtre Page, Mars le capitaine qui conduise vôtre courage; Que vôtre propre monture soit le Pegase ailé, Et Mercure, comme laquais, toujours à vôtre côté." From *La Méthode nouvelle et invention extraordinaire de dresser les chevaux* (Antwerp, 1657), quoted in Guy C. Bauman and Walter A. Liedtke, eds., *Flemish Paintings in America: A Survey of Early Netherlandish and Flemish Paintings in the Public Collections of North America* (Antwerp: Fonds Mercator, 1992), p. 228.
2. See Kristi Nelson, *Jacob Jordaens: Design for Tapestry* ([Turnhout]: Brepols, 1998), pp. 118–32.
3. The art is still practised today, most notably at the Spanish School in Vienna, founded at the end of the sixteenth century and named after the horses who were originally imported from Spain. See also Walter Liedtke, *The Royal Horse and Rider: Painting, Sculpture, and Horsemanship, 1500–1800* (New York: The Metropolitan Museum and Abaris Books, 1989).
4. Antoine de Pluvinel, *Le Maneige Royal* (Paris: 1623).
5. See Julius S. Held, "Jordaens and the Equestrian Anthology," in *Miscellanea Leo van Puyvelde* (Brussels: Éditions de la connaissance, 1949), pp. 153–56.

NICOLAS POUSSIN Landscape with a Woman Washing Her Feet

1. See Claire Pace, *Félibien's Life of Poussin* (London: A. Zwemmer Ltd., 1981), p. 125.
2. Félibien described it as such; see Richard Verdi, ed., *Nicolas Poussin 1594–1665* (London: Royal Academy of Arts and Zwemmer, 1995), no. 69.
3. Small figures and animals used to enliven a landscape or architectural composition.
4. Ann Sutherland Harris, "The subject of Poussin's 'Landscape with a woman bathing' in Ottawa," *The Burlington Magazine* 145 (April 2003): pp. 292–96. The myth is from Ovid *Metamorphoses* 14.623–97, 765–71.
5. Ovid *Fasti* 2.303–59. This translation is from *Ovid's Fasti*, trans. James George Frazer, *The Loeb Classical Library* (Cambridge, Mass., and London: Harvard University Press and William Heinemann Ltd., 1931; reprint, 1967), p. 81.

CAESAR BOETIUS VAN EVERDINGEN The Rape of Europa

1. The United Dutch Provinces were not, of course, a monarchy, and the office of Stadholder (executive officer in The Netherlands) was an elected one, but the office had, over time, become exclusively associated with the noble European house of Orange-Nassau.
2. Ovid *Metamorphoses,* 2.836–75.
3. Paul Huys Janssen, *Caesar van Everdingen 1616/17–1678* (Doornspijk: Davaco Publishers, 2002), no. 54.

GIUSEPPE MARIA CRESPI An Allegory of the Arts

1. Unlike the medieval universities, ancient sources sometimes included such other "arts" as medicine, architecture, and so on.
2. Ovid *Metamorphoses* 10.249–97.

SELECTED BIBLIOGRAPHY

Blankert, Albert, et al. *Dutch Classicism in Seventeenth-Century Painting*. Exh. cat. Rotterdam: Museum Boijmans Van Beuningen, 1999.

Blankert, Albert. *Rembrandt: Genius and His Impact*. Exh. cat. Melbourne: National Gallery of Victoria, 1997.

Brown, Beverly Louise, ed. *The Genius of Rome: 1592–1623*. Exh. cat. London: Royal Academy of Arts, 2001.

Brown, Jonathan, et al. *El Greco of Toledo*. Exh. cat. Boston: Little, Brown and Company, 1982.

Bruyn, J., et al. *A Corpus of Rembrandt Paintings*. 3 vols. Stichting Foundation Rembrandt Research Project. The Hague: M. Nijhoff Publishers, 1982–86.

Davies, David. *El Greco*. Exh. cat. London: National Gallery Company, 2003.

Harris, Ann Sutherland. *Seventeenth-century Art and Architecture*. Upper Saddle River, N.J.: Prentice Hall, 2005.

Hulst, Roger Adolf d', et al. *Jacob Jordaens (1593–1678)*. Exh. cat. Antwerp: Koninklijk Museum voor Schone Kunsten, 1993.

Huys Janssen, Paul. *Caesar van Everdingen 1616/17–1678*. Doornspijk: Davaco Publishers, 2002.

Laskin, Jr., Myron, and Michael Pantazzi, eds. *Catalogue of the National Gallery of Canada, Ottawa: European and American Painting, Sculpture, and Decorative Arts, 1300–1800*. 2 vols. Ottawa: National Gallery of Canada / National Museums of Canada, 1987.

Martin, John Rupert. *Baroque*. London: Alan Lane Penguin Books, 1977.

Spike, John T. *Giuseppe Maria Crespi and the Emergence of Genre Painting in Italy*. Exh. cat. Forth Worth: Kimbell Art Museum, 1986.

Thuillier, Jacques, et al. *Vouet*. Exh. cat. Paris: Éditions de la Réunion des musées nationaux, 1990.

Verdi, Richard, ed. *Nicolas Poussin 1594–1665*. Exh. cat. London: Royal Academy of Arts, 1995.

Vogelaar, Christiaan, et al. *Rembrandt and Lievens in Leiden: "A Pair of Young and Noble Painters."* Exh. cat. Leiden: Stedelijk Museum De Lakenhal, 1991.

White, Christopher. *Peter Paul Rubens: Man and Artist*. New Haven: Yale University Press, 1987.

Whitfield, Clovis, and Jane Martineau, eds. *Painting in Naples 1606–1705: From Caravaggio to Giordano*. Exh. cat. London: Royal Academy of Arts, 1982.

Wood, Jeremy. *Rubens Drawing on Italy*. Exh. cat. Edinburgh: National Gallery of Scotland, 2002.

National Library of Canada Cataloguing in Publication Data

National Gallery of Canada.
Baroque masterworks from the National Gallery of Canada.

Exhibition catalogue.
Issued also in French under title :
Chefs-d'œuvre du baroque du Musée des beaux-arts du Canada.
Includes bibliographical references.
ISBN 0-88884-826-9

1. Painting, Baroque-Europe-Exhibitions. 2. Painting-Ontario-Ottawa-Exhibitions.
3. National Gallery of Canada-Exhibitions. I. Dolphin, Erika II. Title.

ND182 B3 N38 2006 759.04'6
C2006-986003-3

This publication accompanies the exhibition *Baroque Masterworks*, presented by the National Gallery of Canada. All works illustrated are from the collection of the National Gallery of Canada unless otherwise noted. Photographs have been provided by the owners or custodians of the works reproduced unless otherwise noted.

National Gallery of Canada Musée des beaux-arts du Canada

380 Sussex Dr., Ottawa K1N 9N4 http://national.gallery.ca

Cover: Simon Vouet, *The Fortune-teller* (detail), c. 1620 (see p. 10)

Supported by the Department of Canadian Heritage through the Canada Travelling Exhibitions Indemnification Program.

Canadian Heritage Patrimoine canadien

Canada